MW01078810

WHAT OTHERS SAY —

Many thanks for your very well written publication. **Banking With The Beard** is written with the clarity of a natural teacher and with excellent diagrams. Your world-class expertise is presented brilliantly and passionately on every page. This is easily the best book on the subject ever written and will no doubt become a must-have, hands-on learning tool for both novices and "old pros." They'll upgrade their overall game many levels thanks to this veritable "banking Bible" you've given them.

Dick Sussman, Script Writer and Critic

●

Even pros prefer to avoid bank shots – but that may be a thing of the past. **Banking With The Beard** reveals every bit of knowledge necessary to successfully bank to the hole. The addition of great road stories, famous shots, One-Pocket info, and Bank Pool pointers make this book a treasure for serious players.

Tom Shaw, Pool & Billiard Magazine

●

There is simply no over-estimating the value of **Banking With The Beard** for serious players.

George Fels, Billiards Digest

Bank on! brother! The Beard

BANKING WITH THE BEARD

by Freddy Bentivegna

BANKING WITH THE BEARD

Copyright © 2005 Freddy Bentivegna. All Rights Reserved. No part of this book may be reproduced in any form, by any means — electronic, photocopying, recording, digital, DVD or otherwise without written permission. Cover and Diagrams by R Givens.

Dedicated to —

Gene Skinner, of Fullerton, CA, who taught me how to think on a pool table.

Many thanks to George Fels for his kindly instruction in punctuation and grammar.

TABLE OF CONTENTS

CHAPTER SEVEN — MASTER SHOTS & AMAZING MOVES

BANKING WITH THE BEARD
By Freddy Bentivegna

FOREWORD

My name is Freddy Bentivegna, better known in the pool world as "Freddy the Beard." The name goes back to my hippie days when I had long hair, grew a beard and wore a Captain America shirt.

I had misgivings about writing a bank book, because I was reluctant to disclose secrets it took forty years to accumulate. I'm from the "Old School," a place where many pool and billiard secrets went to the grave with their owners.

When I started hanging around the great **Bensingers Billiard Academy** in Chicago information about *how to play* was never bandied about. It was a year before anybody even showed me how to break playing *One-Pocket*.

To get information from a knowledgeable player when I was coming up, you had to buy him breakfast, pay all the time, drop off his cleaning, and for sure drive him home. After all that, he might drop a tiny tidbit of knowledge your way.

The attitude was, "If you are a sucker, stay a sucker, you will get no help from me."

Because of this secretive mind set I stayed a sucker for a long time. I got pummeled mercilessly in **Bensingers** for about three years. I missed plenty of meals and walked home many nights before I got my Pool Hustlers Union Card. Much of what I learned was gleaned from those brutal beatings.

I was so hungry for knowledge that I traveled to Oklahoma City to talk to a dying **Hayden Lingo** and perhaps get a look at his fabled, top-secret, One-Pocket Charts. Hayden Lingo had been a great player who was credited with inventing One-Pocket in the 30s.

Unfortunately, I was too late. Hayden Lingo was already dead.

I tried to pry the Charts from Hayden's widow, but she refused, saying she wasn't sure what she was going to do with his estate. As far as I know, nothing was ever done, and Hayden Lingo's Charts probably wound up in a trash can.

Out of pure meanness, I never intended to explain anything to anybody. I held that attitude until now, when ego has the best of me and I must show the pool world how good my systems really are.

Readers who are discouraged by a thorough discussion of the physics and principles of banks, can jump forward and shoot bank shots according to the Speed and English Charts and the Plus and Minus Charts in the middle of the book (p. 92–98). These Charts will give you a good grasp of the basic principles of banking.

I don't recommend that, however, because players do better when they understand how these things work. When you know how banks work, you can apply the principles in many situations other than those shown in the book. The choice is yours. Either way, you will get a new perspective on how to make bank shots.

Freddy "The Beard" Bentivegna

BANKING WITH THE BEARD

This book explains a simple banking philosophy and a sound banking system. The method is derived from 40 year's of *wrasslin'* with the best bankers in the world for cash money. Crossing cues with great bankers like **Leonard "Bugs" Rucker, John "Cannonball Lefty" Chapman, Alphonso "Fonzi" Daniels, Tony "Fargo" Ferguson, Donny Anderson, Truman Hogue, Billy "Corn Bread Red" Burge, Glenn "Piggy Bank" Rogers, Vernon Eliot, West Side Johnny Boy, "Tough Tony" Brewer, and Kenny "Romberg" Remus**, to name a few, forced me to develop a reliable effective banking system.

This book will eliminate some of the mysteries of banking and make bank shots easier to understand, easier to remember and easier to execute. Banks you view with fear are going to look like "hangers."

We are going to investigate a series of banking angles that keep repeating themselves, and the simple solutions to these angles. We will not entertain the misconception that there are hundreds of different banks to learn and hundreds of different aims, angles and speeds needed to make them.

We are going to study a wonderful bank aiming method based on ideas developed by **"Port Chester Mickey" Carpinello**. "Port Chester Mickey" learned the system from a master player named **William "Sailor" Barge.** What readers will get here is a refined, simplified version of "Sailor" Barge's sighting method that I used in high–stakes competition for many years.

"Sailor" Barge, who had a high run of 356 balls on a *5 x 10* table, was an eccentric champion who snuck around *undercover*, winning local tournaments under assumed names. "Sailor" was a mystery man who kept a low profile up and down the eastern seaboard. *Fifty or no count* on a 5 x 10 was a game he often gave a sucker. "Sailor" was known, and avoided, by all the top players in the East.

Sailor's student, "Port Chester Mickey," was cut from the same bolt of cloth and he eventually became the greatest, unknown player in the country.

The reason Mickey stayed an unknown was his dope habit. Mickey was a heroin addict. He would stay burrowed, deeply, into his dope world for years, never playing a game of pool. Mickey would emerge periodically, when **"Sugar Shack" Johnny Novak** and myself traveled to Port Chester, NY and dragged him out of his drug world and took him with us on the road.

While on the road, Mickey would go "cold turkey" and stay in the room for weeks kicking his habit. "Sugar Shack" insisted that Mickey must be totally straight while he was with us. It usually took about 30 days for Mickey to become a human being again.

After about three weeks, Mickey would start practicing diligently for hours every day. Two weeks of hard practice and he would be ready. Then we would turn him loose on the pool world.

It was like unleashing Dracula on a necklace show. Nobody knew Mickey, so he went through the best players wherever he played like a chain saw going through butter. It was a massacre.

When Mickey was straight he had no bad habits. He didn't drink or smoke and could play for hours on cup of coffee and a candy bar.

Mickey was a brutal sadist on a pool table. He would get ten or twelve games ahead playing 9-Ball (the only game he played) and if his opponent showed the slightest signs of revival, like trying to win a game, Mickey would change the rules in ways that favored him even more — no lucking in the 9-Ball — call your shot, and when he was really feeling ornery he'd make opponents call their position for every shot, which is a test many professionals cannot pass.

Seeing Mickey in action was like watching the 3rd Infantry division rolling through Iraq.

Mickey's position play was so flawless that it seemed that he never had a hard shot. I told him, "I'm not sure if you can really play. You beat everybody, but all you ever shoot is *hangers*."

How good did Mickey really play? Good enough to sneak up on **Wade "Boom Boom" Crane**, aka, **"Billy Johnson"** in Atlanta in the sixties, when Billy only missed an average of one ball a week playing 9-Ball.

When he was off the drugs, Mickey was a clear minded philosopher whose views on any subject were worth recording. With that in mind, I once asked him, "Mickey, with a mind like you have, with such a clear, pure perspective on everything, how the hell could you become a lifetime heroin junkie?"

His reply was a typical Mickeyism, "When I am on heroin, my mind is not so clear."

All things must come to an end. After a few months of looting and pillaging top players, we would wake up one morning and Mickey would be gone. Gone back to Port Chester with his winnings. Gone back to the dope world. Back with freshly healed veins, where the dope, for the first week at least, would actually feel good. Back to no pool and anonymity for a few more years, until "Sugar Shack" and myself would dredge him up again and repeat the ritual.

Hall of Famer **"Iron Joe" Procita** thought enough of Sailor's aiming system to steal it *in toto* and sell it to pool students all over the country in the form of a small cardboard aim finder that was also developed by the Sailor.

If you asked Joe Procita about the top players of the day, Joe would say that he had to spot *all* of them, which he usually did. However, Joe neglected to mention that he also got robbed trying to spot guys like **Johnny "Irish" Lineen**, and the like. Joe didn't think *anybody* could play.

Joe gave Sailor his greatest compliment when he confessed — with his head down — that he couldn't spot Sailor anything. That was Procita's highest praise.

Do not confuse this aiming system with the inaccurate drivel routinely displayed in most instruction books — the imaginary cue-ball system. That nonsense has been pounded into our heads ever since **Willie Mosconi's** instruction book (the red one).

Imaginary cue-ball aiming was even believed and taught by no less then **Irving Crane** as late as the sixties.

Collision–Induced–Throw on the Object Ball was unheard of then. I tried to talk to Crane about throw when we were in *Johnston City, Illinois* in 1964. As great a player as he was — and he could really play — Crane was locked in mentally and wouldn't allow any new concepts into his brain. You could not argue pool theory with Irving Crane.

Crane emphatically stated that if you put an imaginary Cue Ball next to the Object Ball on a direct line to the pocket and you shot the real cue-ball ball into that space, you would have to make the shot.

Of course, we now know that because of **Collision–Induced–Throw** such calculations are not accurate.

Another fruitless argument with Crane was about the stroke required to make one of the corner balls on a 9-Ball break. Crane steadfastly insisted that if the balls were racked correctly it would be impossible to make a corner ball on the break!

Crane based his theory on looking at the 9-Ball rack and noting that the carom angle of the corner balls is aimed at the long rails, not the corner pockets.

Nine–ball players should give thanks to a great player, **"Cannonball Eddie" Kienowski,** from upstate New York, who advanced the theory that if the rack was hit with a certain hard stroke, the whole rack would carry forward about 1/2–inch and *then* open up.

The 1/2-inch forward movement makes the corner ball carom into the corner pocket "on."

Eddie Kienowski explained this to me in the middle sixties in Fort Lauderdale when we were on the road together. I brought it to a few of the great young players of the day, **Jimmy Rempe** of Scranton, Pa., **Jimmy Marino** of Pittsburgh, Pa., **Jimmy Reid** of West Palm Beach, FL., and **Billy Incardona** also of Pittsburgh, when we were all in *Johnston City, Ill.* They were open-minded enough to take full advantage of it.[1]

Crane's 9-Ball break was pitiful — but you certainly couldn't tell him that.

If not for a weak break, I don't know of anyone who would have had an edge on Crane in 9-Ball. Crane ran out perfectly and his safety play was suffocating. He would murder any player whose break wasn't working.

---

[1]Nowadays, with Sardo™ racks guaranteeing a perfect rack every time, every competitive 9-Ball player expects to make one of the corner balls on the break 90+% of the time.

Bud Harris, a great and knowledgeable Three Cushion player from San Francisco, said that good players with wrongheaded notions about ball action unconsciously adjust for erroneous thinking when they aim and during the delivery. Otherwise Crane would have never run so many balls.

Misconceptions about the physics of billiards are not uncommon among better players. Some have almost no idea of how things work. They just know that doing something a certain way succeeds. Despite their flat earth theories, many of them can play very well indeed.

Back to the imaginary Cue Ball concept. Some books add a little proviso to this worthless method by mentioning **Collision–Induced–Throw**, which is good. But their explanations fall short when they merely say, "Cut the ball a little more to allow for throw."

These writers never bother to tell the reader how much of an adjustment is needed. An inch? A foot? A mile? No one, until "Sailor" Barge, has addressed exactly where to aim at the Object Ball with the throw figured in.

Our system is based on aiming with the center of the tip of the cue-stick. We are going to break the Object Ball up into seven parts and seven different aims. The original system Sailor himself used broke the ball up into sixteen parts and sixteen aims! We are not going to go that strong. Such fine increments of aiming are practical only for monsters like "Sailor" and aliens from Mars.

For normal humans, seven aims are plenty. As a matter of fact, for my bank system we are going to be able to limit our study to only five basic aims. The other two aims will be shown, but they apply to regular straight–in pool only.

I have digressed from the theme of this book — a winning bank pool system — but I wanted to provide some background on where this aiming method came from. Without further ado, here for your enjoyment is a goodly chunk of my bank pool knowledge. I wish you good luck with it.

VACILLATING VARIABLES

Quite a few competing variables affect bank shots:

Firmness of the cushions. The firmer the cushion the sharper the angle of rebound. Billiard tables generally have softer cushions than pool tables. That's why systems that work well on billiard tables often produce considerably different results on pool tables. The firmness of the cushions varies from table to table and must be taken into account to get accurate results.

Condition of the cloth. The newer or fuzzier the cloth the wider the rebound angle tends to be. New or fuzzy cloth also has less effect ball action than older or rougher cloth and the Cue Ball retains english and draw longer on new cloth, but the effects of ball action are less due to the smaller amount of friction on the cloth for the ball to react against. This sometimes causes a catch-22 situation where you have more backspin on impact,   but get a shorter draw or less effect for the amount of english used.

Surface texture of the balls. New balls or balls that are kept clean or just polished have less friction, reducing the effects of ball action. Old balls with surface marks or balls that are just plain dirty have more friction, increasing the effects of ball to ball action. The extra friction alters bank angles and has more effect on the bed cloth as well.

Humidity.   When the cloth is damp, the initial effect of any type of ball action is more pronounced. However, damp cloth has more friction, so the Cue Ball (or Object Ball) loses ball action sooner than on dry cloth. This causes players to think they get less action off the rails when it is damp, but careful observation shows that the amount of english actually left at the moment of contact has a greater effect than when the table is dry.

Friction.   As a general rule, any condition that increases friction magnifies the immediate effects of ball action off the cushions. Much of the ball action may be lost due to the friction of the cloth on the way to the rail, but whatever is remains causes a bigger change in rebound angle than otherwise.

This is an important point to keep in mind when Object Balls are close to a cushion where the ball retains most of the action imparted to it until contact, which is where it counts in banks.

Ball action. Draw, follow, english and speed are variables themselves, and can change bank angles considerably, depending on the amount used. Moreover, draw, follow, english and force interact, amplifying or canceling each other out. The effects of ball action must be taken into account to bank accurately.

All in all, playing on new equipment when the weather's warm and dry is a great deal different than when the balls are gummy, the rails are sticky, the bed cloth is sandpapery and it is damp as hell. Experts usually adjust to varying conditions better than average players, but when conditions are extreme, even professionals have trouble adapting.

General condition of the table. Tables that are out of level, have rips in the cloth, poorly adjusted cushions and balls that came down from the Middle Ages are unplayable and a real game of pool is never seen on them. Some tables have such weird playing conditions that it is impossible to do more than predict the general direction a ball will take off a cushion and even that isn't easy.

Most tables are off a little, but the equipment I am talking about gives champions a brain fever trying to adjust. Dealing with extreme conditions teaches very little other than how bad a table can be, so I recommend finding decent equipment to play on.

Study and Practice Necessary. It should be clear that students are going to have to study the systems and get on the table and practice the lessons to benefit from this book. Merely reading about a system and running the numbers through your mind won't succeed. Even simple methods for calculating banks require some familiarity to use them well.

As a king of France was told when trying to find an easy way to learn a complex subject "There is no royal road to learning."

All a teacher can do is point the student in the right direction. Practice and study of the billiard principles involved in bank shots is necessary to become a good banker.

With these thoughts in mind, let's assume that playing conditions are fairly close to what would be considered "good." Then some reasonably accurate statements can be made about banks.

KEY TO ILLUSTRATIONS

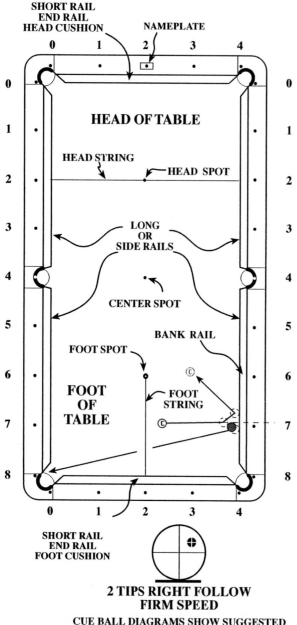

SHORT RAIL
END RAIL
HEAD CUSHION

NAMEPLATE

HEAD OF TABLE

HEAD STRING

HEAD SPOT

LONG
OR
SIDE RAILS

CENTER SPOT

BANK RAIL

FOOT SPOT

FOOT
OF
TABLE

FOOT
STRING

SHORT RAIL
END RAIL
FOOT CUSHION

2 TIPS RIGHT FOLLOW
FIRM SPEED

CUE BALL DIAGRAMS SHOW SUGGESTED
SPEEDS AND STRIKING POINTS.

The illustrations represent a 4–1/2 x 9 foot (50" x 100") table drawn to exact scale.

The Diamonds divide the space between the noses of the cushions into equal parts. On a 4–1/2 x 9 foot table, the Diamonds are 12.5 inches apart.

The Diamonds are used as aids in aiming banks

The Zero – Four – Eight Diamond positions on the long rails and the Zero – Four Diamond positions on the short rails are shown in all illustrations.

**BLACK BALLS SHOW
ORIGINAL POSITIONS**

**GREY BALLS SHOW
MOVED POSITIONS**

**DASHED BALLS SHOW
CONTACT POINTS
ON OBJECT BALLS AND
CUSHIONS**

**BLACK LINES SHOW
SHOT PATH**

**DASHED LINES SHOW
ALIGNMENTS AND SIGHT LINES**

DIVIDING THE ANGLE

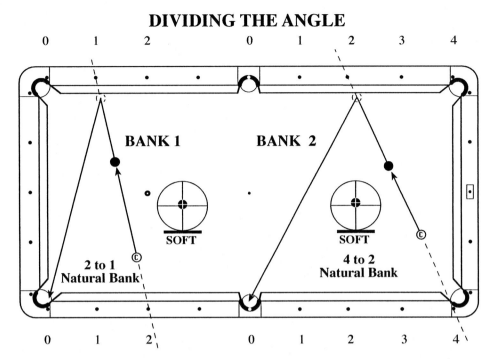

The illustration above shows the simple 2 to 1 banking system that will be used as a reference for many one–cushion bank shots. This method is commonly called "dividing the angle" or "bisecting the angle." Banks are figured by extending the bank lines through the Diamonds and dividing the distance to the target by 2.

If merely calculating the correct bank angle were the only problem in making banks, we'd be done now. Unfortunately, even the simple banks shown here will only score when played with the right blend of english, speed, and Cut Angle. If the bank is hit with the wrong speed or the Object Ball must be cut into the correct path or english is used for position play, the bank no longer scores unless these changes are accounted for.

My system shows you how to control the interplay of contrary variables that affect every bank shot.

BANKING WITH THE BEARD
AIMS

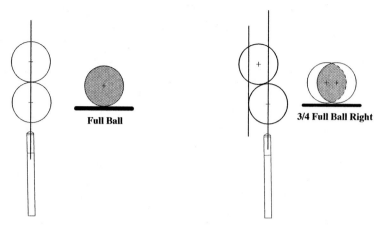

To keep calculations as simple as possible, this system uses only nine aims (counting left and right cuts) on the Object Ball for solving banks.

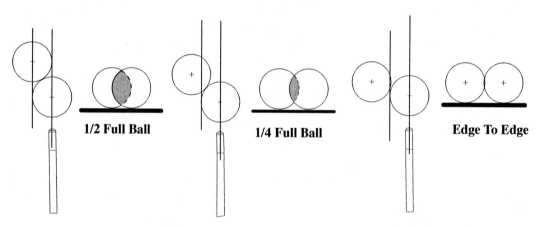

Limiting the number of aims used on the Object Ball provides a rational basis for linking the effects of *Acquired English, Cut Angle, Fullness of Hit* and *Transferred english* to accurately control rebound angles.

Naturally, when cutting to the opposite side, you should reverse the aiming process.

3/4 FULL BALL AIM

Look directly at the Object Ball as though you were lining up a straight–in shot, but only cover 3/4 of the Object Ball with the Cue Ball.

This is how a 3/4 Full Aim looks in straight–in pool.

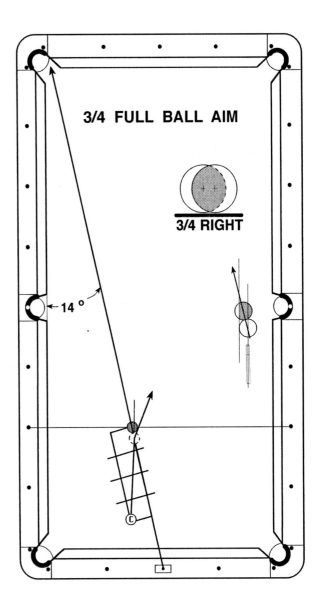

3/4 FULL BALL AIM

3/4 RIGHT

14 °

1/2 FULL BALL AIM

Look directly at the Object Ball as though you were lining up a straight-in shot, but only cover 1/2 of the Object Ball with the Cue Ball

Another way of lining up a 1/2 Full hit is to point the tip of the cue through the center of the Cue Ball and aim at the outer edge of the Object Ball.

This is how a 1/2 Full Ball hit looks in straight-in pool.

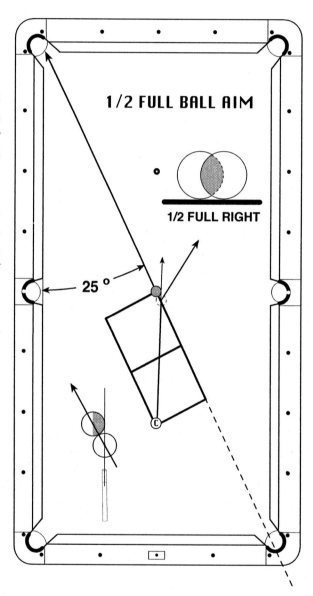

1/4 FULL BALL AIM

Here's another way to determine fullness of hit.

Look directly at the Object Ball as though you were lining up a straight–in shot, then cover 1/4 of the Object Ball with the Cue Ball.

The example shows how a 1/4 Full Ball Aim looks in straight-in pool.

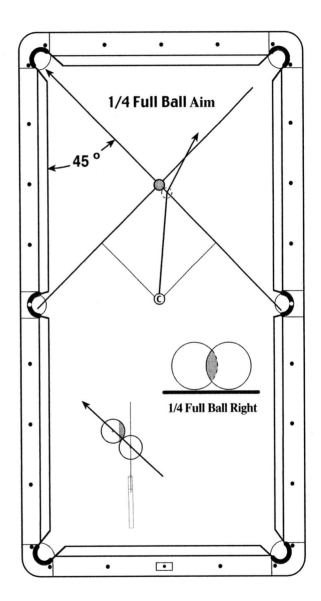

1/4 Full Ball Aim

45°

1/4 Full Ball Right

5/6 FULL BALL AIM

Look directly at the Object Ball as though you were lining up a dead straight–in shot. But only cover 5/6 of the Object Ball with the Cue Ball.

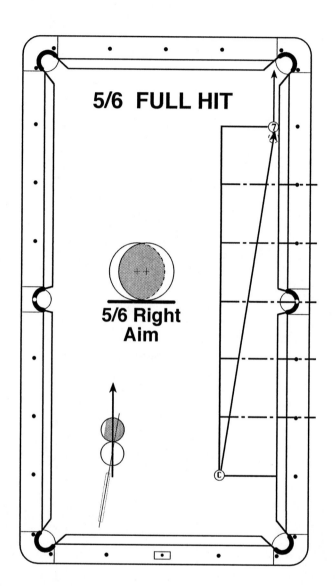

1/3 FULL BALL AIM

Look directly at the Object Ball as though you were lining up a dead straight–in shot.

But only cover 1/3 of the Object Ball with the Cue Ball.

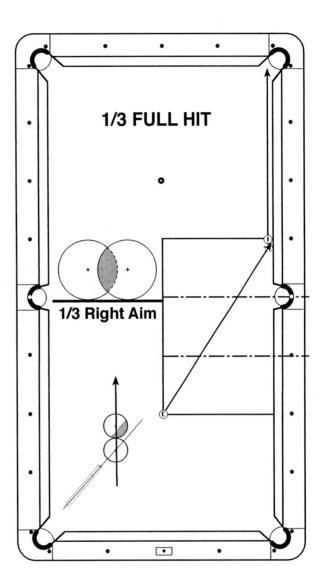

1/3 FULL HIT

1/3 Right Aim

EFFECTS OF SPEED

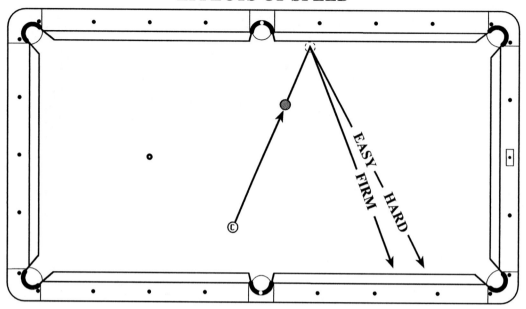

The effects of speed are readily apparent. As a ball is hit harder, the rebound angle becomes shorter.

Since speed is infinitely variable, we will confine ourselves to using three defined velocities — **Easy**, **Firm** and **Hard**.

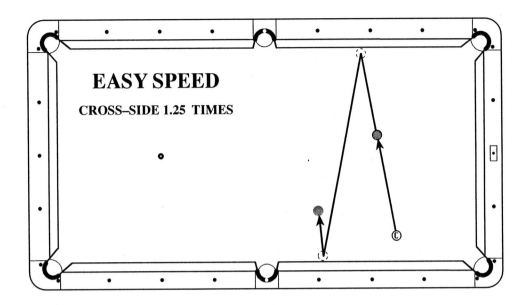

EASY SPEED

CROSS–SIDE 1.25 TIMES

To simplify our calculations, we only use three **Measured Speeds** to control banks — **Easy**, **Firm** and **Hard**. Using three specific speeds reduces the complexities of velocity by producing predictable changes in bank angle that are figured in our calculations. Using variables with known values and known effects enables us to substitute variables to achieve position play and still make the bank.

Easy Speed provides enough force to drive an Object Ball about 1.25 times cross–side.

An inherent problem in determining bank speed is the question of relative distance. Common sense must be used, because the closer the Cue Ball is to the Object Ball, the less force it takes to hit the shot **Firm** or **Hard**. With less distance, the Cue Ball loses less speed before contact. Conversely, the farther apart the balls are the easier it is to hit the ball **Easy**.

What we are talking about is the friction of the cloth that reduces Cue Ball and Object Ball speeds.

You, as a player, have to use judgement to achieve **Hard**, **Firm** or **Easy** bank speeds. Practice and instinct will guide you.

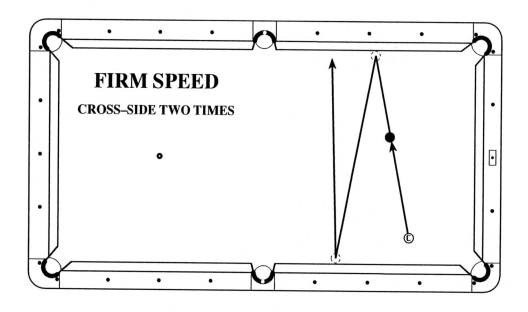

FIRM SPEED

CROSS–SIDE TWO TIMES

FIRM is enough speed to send the Object Ball cross–side two times.

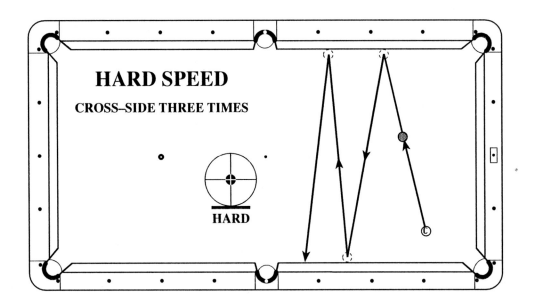

HARD SPEED

CROSS–SIDE THREE TIMES

HARD

Here's what is meant by **Hard Speed**. A **Hard** stroke sends the Object Ball across table three times as shown.

MEASURED ENGLISH

One Tip Follow

One Tip Left English   **Center Ball**   **One Tip Right English**

One Tip Draw

Two Tips Follow

Two Tips Left English   **Two Tips Right English**

Two Tips Draw

It is crystal-clear that we must account for any english we use when banking a ball, because of its profound effect on the bank path.

This chart shows how we will measure english in this method of sighting banks. *Tips of english* will be applied as shown above.

In order to avoid nightmare calculations involving the full gamut of english, we will apply spin to the Cue Ball in predetermined amounts, measured in Tips as shown here.

In this system, **1 Tip of English** equals **1/4 Diamond** on the rail or a **1/4 Ball Cut** on the Object Ball.

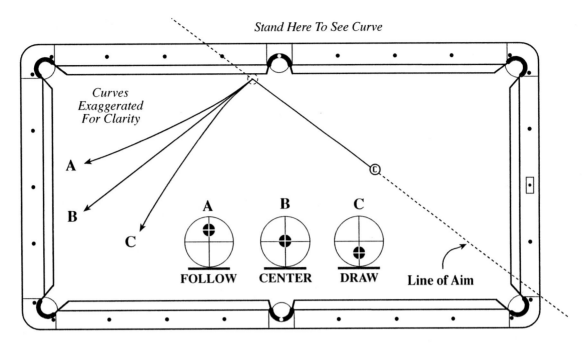

Draw and Follow affect rebound angles, and must be accounted for to accomplish accurate banking.

Draw shortens the bank angle and Follow causes the Cue Ball to run long. Rotation applied to the Cue Ball causes it to curve after leaving the cushion. Stand near the cushion, and you can see the Cue Ball curve as it leaves the cushion.

Center Ball tends to produce a geometrically equal bank angle, providing the shot is not hit too hard or too softly so the Cue Ball begins rolling before contact. The Cue Ball must be *sliding* at the instant of contact with the cushion to produce an equal bank angle.

The same principles apply to Object Balls, the only difference being that an Object Ball cannot acquire nearly as much spin as a Cue Ball struck with a cue tip.

The thing that counts in banks is the action a ball has at the moment of impact with the cushion, not what it started with. If the Center Ball and Draw shots are hit too softly and lose their slide or backspin to the friction of the cloth before hitting the cushion, the ball acts as though it has Follow because it does. A rolling ball is a rolling ball, no matter how it began.

ENGLISH

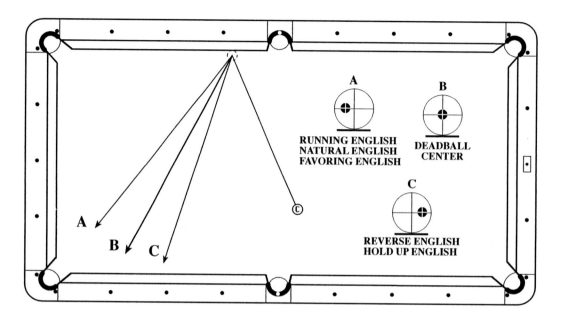

The effects of english on cushion shots are immediate and obvious to see.

A: Running English widens the bank angle.

B: Center Ball tends to produce an equal bank. The Cue Ball must be sliding without any rotation at the instant of contact and without excessive force to create an equal rebound angle.

C: Reverse or Hold–Up English opposes the direction of the bank, shortening the bank angle and slowing the ball somewhat.

Not much needs to be said about these easy-to-understand principles of banking, but every bank shot must account for the effects of english to score.

Put up the money *before* every session —
and have somebody *you* know hold the stakes.

Get paid after *every* game and don't sleep no scratches.

Roy "Kilroy" Kosmolski's Rules Of The Road

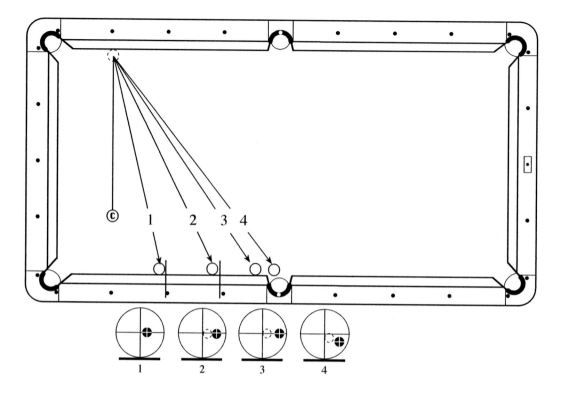

Unless you've been in a coma most of your life, you know that english deflects the Cue Ball to the side the spin is applied to when the ball hits a cushion. To wit: Right–English sends the Cue Ball to the right, and vice versa for Left–English.

What ordinary players do not know is exactly how much change in bank angle there will be with any specific amount of english.

INSIDE and OUTSIDE ENGLISH

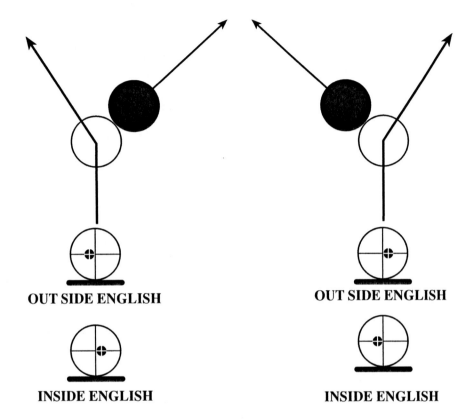

OUT SIDE ENGLISH   OUT SIDE ENGLISH

INSIDE ENGLISH   INSIDE ENGLISH

This is what is meant when the terms **Inside** and **Outside English** are used in this book. **Outside English** is applied on the side of the Cue Ball away from the direction of the cut on the Object Ball.

This is to say, when we cut a ball to the right, Left English will be **Outside English** and Right English will be **Inside English**.

Likewise, when we cut a ball to the left, Right English will be **Outside English** and Left English will be **Inside English**.

TRANSMITTED ENGLISH

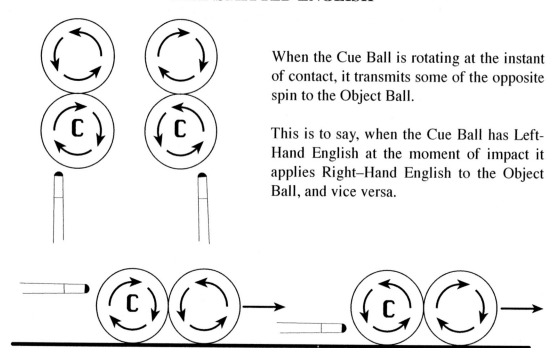

When the Cue Ball is rotating at the instant of contact, it transmits some of the opposite spin to the Object Ball.

This is to say, when the Cue Ball has Left-Hand English at the moment of impact it applies Right–Hand English to the Object Ball, and vice versa.

The same principle is at work when the Cue Ball has draw or follow on contact. This is to say, Draw puts a small amount of Follow on the Object Ball while Follow generates a tiny amount of Draw on the Object Ball.

We can regard the interaction between a rotating Cue Ball and an Object Ball as the meshing of cog wheels which naturally turn in opposite directions.

Needless to say, the smooth surfaces of billiard balls do not transfer spin with anywhere near the efficiency of a gear, because a good deal of spin is lost to slippage during the collision.[1] Nonetheless, transmitted english has a profound effect on bank angles

---

[1]According to Robert Byrne, clean polished balls only transmit about 2% of Cue Ball spin to an Object Ball with a Full Hit. With dirty balls, considerably more spin can be transmitted.
Byrne's Complete Book of Pool Shots © 2003, P. 92

PROOF of TRANSMITTED ENGLISH

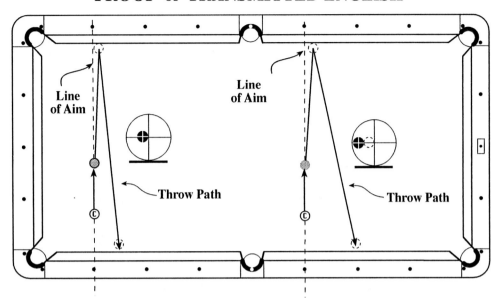

This exercise settles any doubts about transmitting english to Object Balls.

Some cantankerous sorts, who also like to argue flat-earth theories just to aggravate sensible people, maintain that an Object Ball cannot have enough english applied during the collision to significantly affect a shot. These unobservant souls claim that the phenomena we plainly see is actually an optical illusion concealing the fact that the Cue Ball curved before impact, changing the ball's trajectory without Throwing the ball or applying any spin to it.

The objections of these feckless nit-pickers cannot withstand the simple demonstration above which proves that enough Throw and English can be applied to an Object Ball to deflect the bank path a full Diamond space or more going cross side. One Tip of english applies enough side-spin to change the Object Ball rebound angle about 6 degrees, or 1/2 Diamond space. Using Two Tips of English changes a square hit 12 degrees or even more.

The Object Ball is definitely Thrown to the side during the collision, and a small amount of english is applied to the ball that can easily be seen acting on the cushion when you get the right mix of speed and spin.

The exact amount of Transmitted English depends on the friction between the balls. New, highly polished balls exhibit considerably less Throw than older balls that are worn and have surface defects.

ACQUIRED ENGLISH

Size of Flattened Area

1/16"	1/8"	1/4"	5/16"	3/8"

Soft	Moderate	Hard	Very Hard	King Kong??

For players with inquiring minds, a few simple experiments will greatly expand your understanding of the role cut–angle plays in applying english to Object Balls.

The first step is to establish a rational basis for imparting english to an Object Ball, even though the Cue Ball is rolling or sliding without sidespin.

Get some carbon paper and tape a piece to an Object Ball, carbon side out.

Now hit the carbon paper with the Cue Ball. A circular marking will be imprinted on the Cue Ball. (The carbon mark is easy to remove later.) The diameter of this circle indicates the flattened area between the balls during the collision. The harder the collision, the bigger the flattened area

 It is readily seen that the contact area between the balls is never a pinpoint, even at slow speeds. As the velocity of the impact increases, the diameter of the flattened area rapidly grows to 1/8" and then to 1/4" with a moderately hard stroke.

The restitution of the balls is proclaimed on every shot by the snap when the balls spring apart. All the noise of two balls colliding is generated in a distance of about 0.010" as the balls separate. That's how far the flattened surfaces of the balls spring back to restore their spherical shape.

Now let's see how flattening and the Acquired English it enables affects ball action.

ACQUIRED ENGLISH

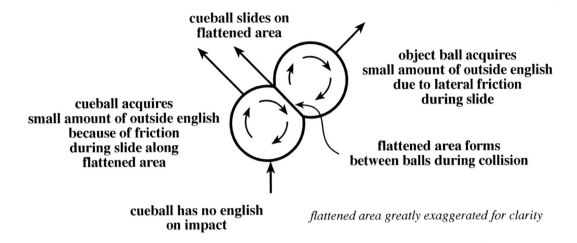

cueball slides on
flattened area

object ball acquires
small amount of outside english
due to lateral friction
during slide

cueball acquires
small amount of outside english
because of friction
during slide along
flattened area

flattened area forms
between balls during collision

cueball has no english
on impact

flattened area greatly exaggerated for clarity

LATERAL SLIDE CREATES ENGLISH and/or THROWS Object Ball

The diagram above illustrates the fundamental principle that makes it possible to transmit english from the Cue Ball to an Object Ball. During an angular collision, a flattened area forms between the balls and the Cue Ball *slides* along this flattened area for a brief instant in time, imparting a small measure of angular rotation and/or Throw to the Object Ball.

Once the mechanism for producing *Acquired English* is understood, the calculus for figuring the amount of english generated during an angular collision can be figured.

With fuller hits, less english is generated because there is very little lateral slide and very little **Collision-Induced-English** is created. As the collision angle grows, the amount of *Acquired English* increases — up to a point. Some english is applied to the Object Ball even on the thinnest of hits.

The unique thing about *Acquired English* is that both the Cue Ball and Object Ball leave the collision with the same english. This is to say Outside English (away from the direction of the cut). Although the amount of english induced is relatively small, it is enough to change rebound angles by 1/2 diamond or even more.

Failing to account for collision-generated side-spin and Throw causes misses in bank pool.

Now we will continue with a practical discussion on how to cope with *Acquired English* on Cut Banks and Passover Banks.

ACQUIRED ENGLISH

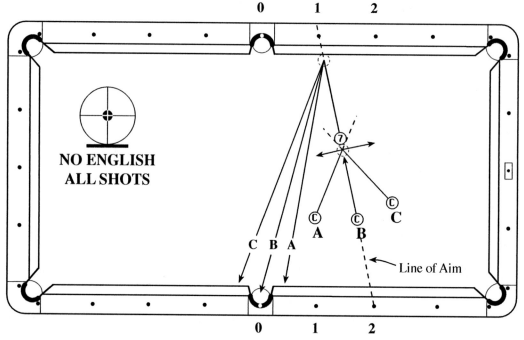

Many players never realize that cutting an Object Ball at an angle always generates a small amount of english and/or *Throw* on both the Object Ball and Cue Ball even when the Cue Ball has zero side-spin on impact.

Most bank systems assume that all of the shots above will score by merely driving the Object Ball into the cushion on the line of aim. However, when you actually shoot these shots you will find more than a half-diamond difference in the bank path from position A to position C.

The reason for this divergence is that the Object Ball *"acquires"* a small, but significant, amount of spin and the ball is *Thrown* during the collision. Only Example B will score without adjusting for *Acquired English* (aka— **Collision–Induced–English**)

Failing to account for **Collision–Induced–English** introduces an error into the calculation for every Cut or Passover Bank because enough english can be *acquired* by an Object Ball during a collision to deflect the ball more than 1/2 diamond off the natural bank line on a cross-table shot. The changes in rebound angles caused by *Acquired English* make it essential to include this subtle but vital aspect of ball action in our calculations.

ACQUIRED ENGLISH VARIES WITH CUT ANGLE

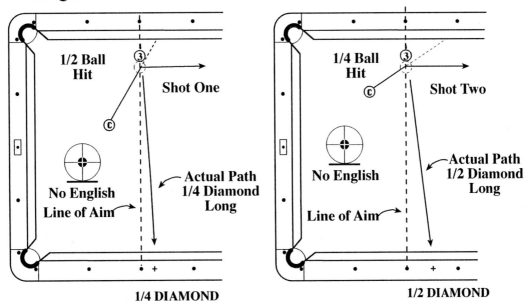

This simple exercise demonstrates the effects of *Acquired English* on angular collisions. In both cases above, the Object Ball "*acquires*" a small amount of Right–Hand english during the collision that deflects the ball as much as 1/2 diamond off a true path.

With a 1/2 ball hit, the Object Ball is Thrown 1/4 diamond off a true course on the rebound.

Using a 1/4 ball hit sends the Object Ball 1/2 diamond off the geometric course.

This system predicts the combined effects of spin and throw for a particular hit, not exactly how the individual components contribute to the rebound angle.

For the moment, satisfy yourself that *Acquired English* is a fact to reckon with when playing banks. We'll get into the details later.

REMOVING ACQUIRED ENGLISH

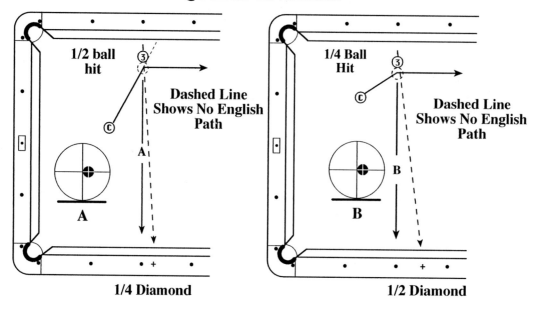

Acquired English can be eliminated by applying enough Outside English to the Cue Ball to cancel the friction between the balls during the collision.

Theoretically, an amount of Outside English equal to the amount of english that would be *Acquired* at a given angle will erase **Collision-Induced–English** and **Throw**, and the Object Ball will take a more geometric path.

As a practical matter **1 Tip of Outside English** is enough to eliminate **Collision-Induced–English** and **Throw**.

ENHANCING ACQUIRED ENGLISH

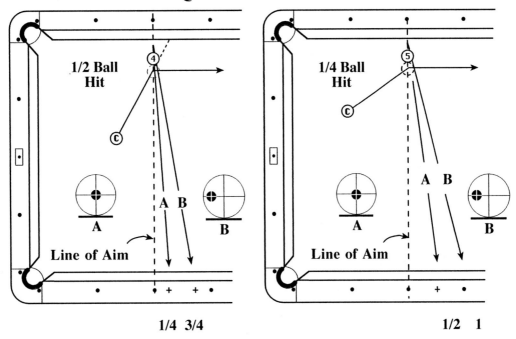

Acquired English can also be enhanced by using Inside English.

Learning to control **Collision-Induced-English** is necessary to accurately control the path of the banked ball.

EFFECTS OF ENGLISH APPLIED TO THE CUE BALL

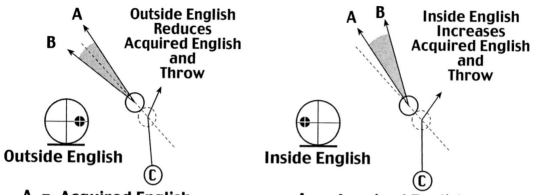

A = Acquired English   A = Acquired English
B = Outside English Path   B = Inside English

Angles Exaggerated For Clarity

OUTSIDE ENGLISH

Players can increase or decrease the amount of *Acquired English* an Object Ball has when it departs from the collision by applying Inside or Outside English to the Cue Ball.

Using Outside English (Right–Hand English in this example) reduces or eliminates the friction between the balls, decreasing *Acquired English*. If enough Outside English is used, **Collision-Induced–English** and **Throw** can be overcome entirely and the Object Ball throws to the left.

INSIDE ENGLISH

Inside English adds to *Acquired English*, increasing **Throw**, and adds to the amount of english applied to the Object Ball.

Observation tells us that Inside English has a greater effect in throwing the Object Ball away from the geometric line between the centers of the balls at the instant of impact.

The reason for this difference is that some of the Outside English is used up overcoming the **Collision–Induced–Throw** before any throw caused by the Outside English can occur. Some Outside English is subtracted before it has any effect. Inside English suffers no reduction of effect during the collision because it is simply **added** to the **Collision–Induced–Throw**.

Inside English increases the friction during the lateral slide, producing a greater effect than Outside English at the same angle and speed.

INFINITE POSSIBILITIES?

Serious bank players readily understand the importance of including **Collision–Induced–English** and the english applied to the Cue Ball in their calculations.

Obviously, if we can control the angle at which a ball leaves the cushion, with we're on our way to stellar banking.

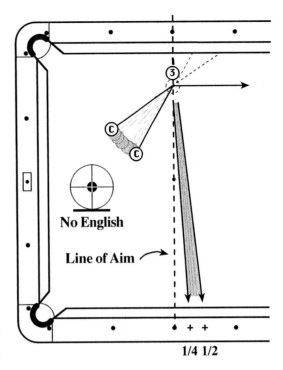

Unfortunately, there are an infinite number of Cut Angles between a **1/4 Ball Hit** and a **1/2 Ball Hit**. It would require infinite variations in english to exactly compensate for all of them, because every tiny increment in Cut Angle generates a proportional change in the amount of *Acquired English* and the deflection off a cushion.

If we try to cope with **Collision-Induced-English** on a case-by-case basis, a million tiny increments of english and speed would be needed to create the desired bank angles. Add the full gamut of the effects of draw, follow and applied english into the mix, and the formula for solving banks quickly becomes so complicated that it would take a mainframe computer to solve the nightmare equations.

Don't panic, because I'm going to crunch all of these variables into a much simpler and a much more understandable approach that integrates the effects of speed, english, Cut Angle (*Acquired English*), transferred english (applied to the Cue Ball) and bank angle into an easy to understand equation that enables us to reliably make one-cushion banks.

To bring order out of the chaos of infinite Cut Angles, infinite speeds and infinite shifts in *Acquired English*, we must eliminate the uncertainties in our calculations by reducing the dozens of possible variables used to aim and score banks to a much simpler package.

Instead of sighting banks with infinite Cut Angles, we will limit ourselves to **1/4-Ball** increments, and we will only use specific speeds and specific amounts of english that produce known results.

Now we'll get into the tools and methods needed to make solving banks simpler and more reliable.

Now I'm going to blend all of this information into a tasty aiming system.

We'll begin by exploring some useful options for Natural, Straight–In, 2-to-1 Bank Angles.

NATURAL BANKS

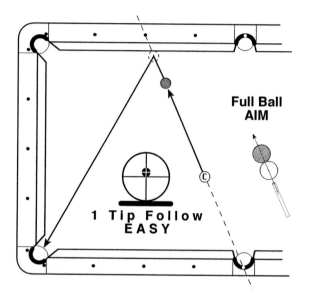

SOLUTION 1
Aim to hit the Object Ball full in the face using 1 Tip of Follow with an **EASY** stroke.

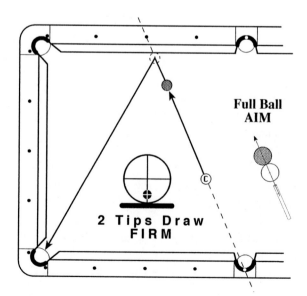

SOLUTION 2
Aim to hit the Object Ball full in the face using 2 Tips of Draw with a **FIRM** stroke.

SOLUTION 3

Aim to hit the Object Ball full in the face using One Tip of Outside English with a **FIRM** stroke.

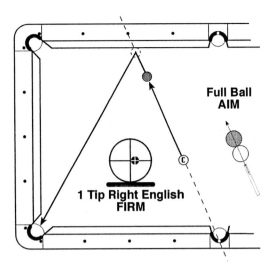

Full Ball AIM

1 Tip Right English FIRM

SOLUTION 4

Aim to hit the Object Ball full in the face using Two Tips of Outside English with a **HARD** stroke.

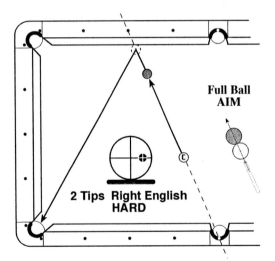

Full Ball AIM

2 Tips Right English HARD

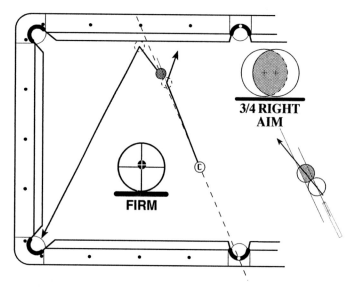

SOLUTION 5

Aim to hit the Object Ball **3/4 Full** using a **FIRM** stroke.

THE GOLDEN NUGGET

Here's the fun part. These solutions for Straight-On, Natural Banks work all over the table. When we land on a Natural 2:1 angle, be it a cross-corner, a cross-side or a straight-back bank, we can use several options to make the shot and play position. We can consolidate what seemed to be dozens of different shots into a five shot position package.

This is the thought sequence for all Natural, Straight–On, Full-In-The-Face Banks. First determine if the Object Ball and the Cue Ball lie on a Natural 2 to 1 angle. Next, depending on the position needed, fit the bank into one of the five options we have just covered.

Use english in **1-Tip** increments to get position and to make the bank.

Now we come to the golden nugget of this system. This is the gem of wisdom you paid for. **One Tip of English** equals about **1/4 Diamond** or a **1/4 Ball Hit**. We can interchange these variables by hitting the Object Ball **1/4 Fuller** or **Thinner**, or by adding or subtracting **1/4 Diamond** from the aim or by applying an appropriate amount of english measured in **Tips**.

CUT BANKS

Now we'll examine some Cut Banks and their solutions. The first point to remember is that Cut Banks tend to land about 1/4 Diamond short of the mark when played with **Firm Speed**.

Cut Bank 1

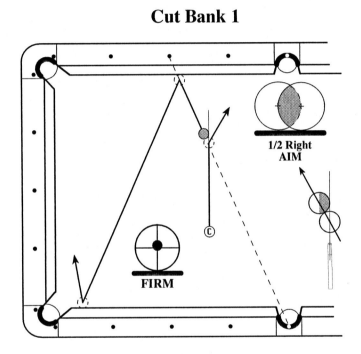

Cut Bank 1

When a Cut Bank is played directly into the Natural 2:1 bank with **Firm Speed,** the shot tends to land about 1/4 Diamond short, due to **Collision–Induced–Throw** and *Acquired English*.

Solution 1

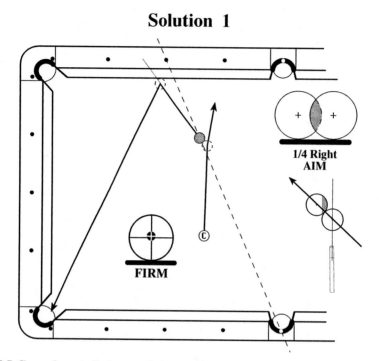

Using **FIRM Speed** and **Subtracting 1/4 Ball** from the hit adjusts the bank to score.

Solution 2

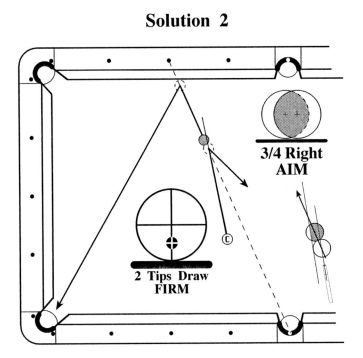

3/4 Right
AIM

2 Tips Draw
FIRM

The bank angle can also be corrected by using **Two Tips of Draw** with **FIRM Speed**.

Solution 3

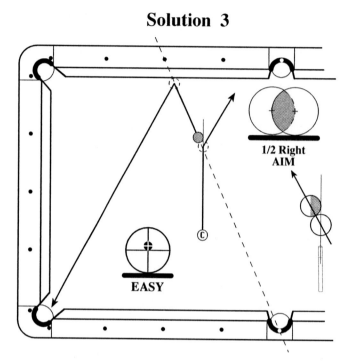

1/2 Right
AIM

EASY

The bank angle can also be corrected with a Center Hit and **Easy Speed**.

Solution 4

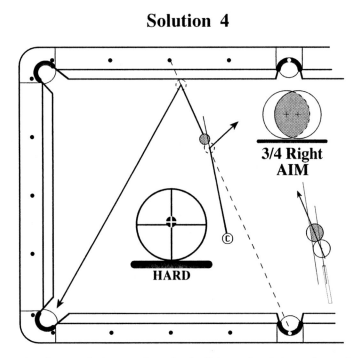

This bank can also be made by cutting the ball into the 2:1 angle and using a **HARD** stroke.

Speed kills action and the **Collision–Induced–Throw** is negated by sheer force, sending the ball into the pocket.

Cut Banks work best using One-Half Tip of High or Low Ball to keep the Object Ball from sliding and changing the rebound angle.

PASSOVER BANKS

Now we'll examine some **Passover Banks** and their solutions.

3/4 Passover Bank

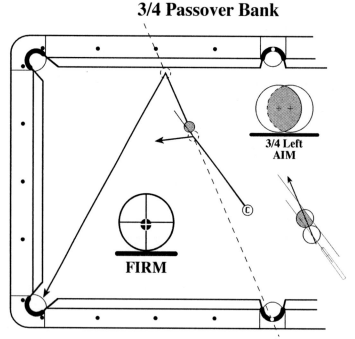

3/4 Left
AIM

FIRM

3/4 Passover Bank — 1

When a **Passover Bank** is played directly into the Natural 2:1 bank angle **Easy, Firm** and **Hard Speeds** all work.

Easy Speed scores because the reduced speed allows **Collision–Induced–Throw** to wear off and the Object Ball takes a Natural 2:1 Angle.

Firm Speed pockets the bank because enough **Collision–Induced–Throw** is acquired to make the angle work.

Shooting Hard also sends the Object Ball into the pocket, the reason being that speed kills action and the **Collision–Induced–Throw** is negated by sheer force so it has little effect.

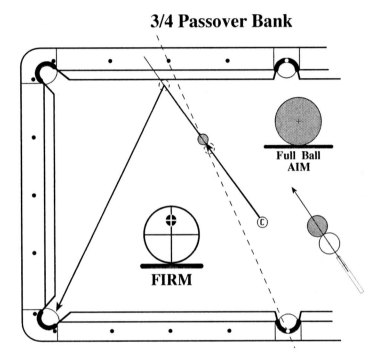

3/4 Passover Bank

Full Ball AIM

FIRM

3/4 Passover Bank — 2

Adding 1/4 Ball to the hit and using **2 Tips Follow** with a **FIRM** stroke adjusts the bank to score.

In this case, a **Full Ball Hit** does the job.

Rather than cutting the Object Ball into the **2:1 Natural Angle**, we use a **Full Hit** with **2 Tips of Follow**. The follow action shortens the bank path.

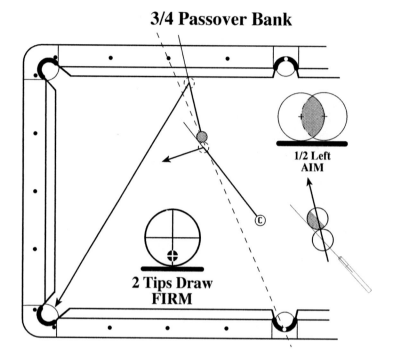

3/4 Passover Bank

1/2 Left
AIM

2 Tips Draw
FIRM

3/4 Passover Bank — 3
Subtracting **1/4 Ball** from the hit and using **2 Tips Draw** with a **FIRM** stroke adjusts the bank to score.

This time, a **1/2 Full Ball Hit** does the job.

3/4 Passover Bank

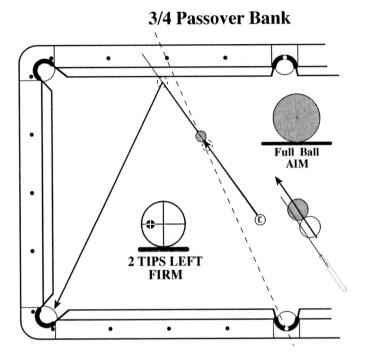

Full Ball AIM

2 TIPS LEFT FIRM

3/4 Passover Bank — 4

Add 1/4 Ball to the hit — 3/4 + 1/4 = Full Ball Hit.

Two Tips of Left-English with a **FIRM** stroke shortens the bank angle 1/4 Diamond to score.

1/2 Passover Bank

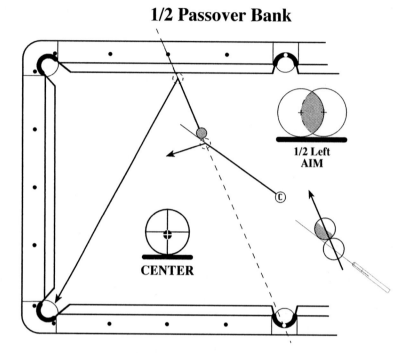

1/2 Passover Bank — 5

When a **1/2 Ball Hit** is required for the Natural Bank Angle, you can score using **Easy**, **Firm** and **Hard Speeds**.

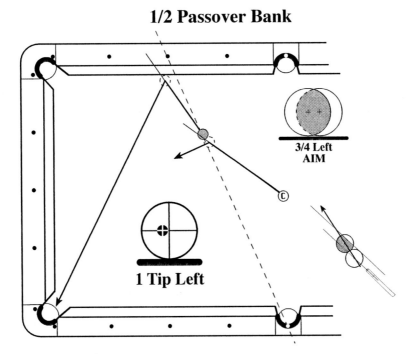

1/2 Passover Bank — 6

A **3/4 Ball Hit** with **1 Tip of Reverse English** and **FIRM** speed can also be used to score.

The **Reverse English** throws the Object Ball and applies a small amount of opposing english to the Object Ball that corrects the bank angle.

1/2 Passover Bank

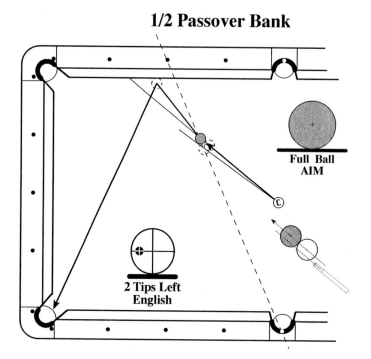

Full Ball
AIM

2 Tips Left
English

Passover Bank — 7

When a 1/2 Ball Hit is required for the Natural Bank Angle you can also use a Full Ball Hit with 2 Tips of Reverse English and **FIRM Speed** to score.

The Reverse English corrects the bank angle by **Throwing** the Object Ball closer to the proper angle and by applying a small amount of opposing english to the Object Ball that shortens the bank to a scoring path.

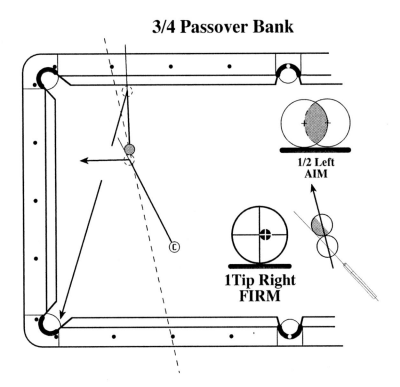

3/4 Passover Bank

1/2 Left
AIM

1Tip Right
FIRM

3/4 Passover Bank — 8

A 3/4 Full Hit is required to drive the Object Ball onto the 2-to-1 path. Subtracting 1/4 ball for a **1/2 Full Hit** and using **1 Tip of Right English** combined with the **Collision–Induced–Throw** sends this workhorse One–Pocket bank into your pocket.

Use **Firm Speed.**

SIDE–STEP BANK (Partial Passover)

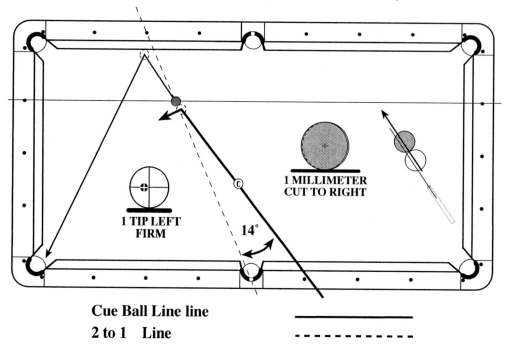

1 MILLIMETER
CUT TO RIGHT

1 TIP LEFT
FIRM

14°

Cue Ball Line line _____

2 to 1   Line - - - - - - - - - -

Learning the **Side–Step Bank** is a mighty addition to any banker's repertoire, because after you learn this bank the odds are better than 19-1 that you will make the shot wherever and whenever it comes up.

Take a good look at the diagram above because it illustrates the secret of the **Side–Step Bank** in graphic terms. The first important point to note is the 14° angle between the 2 to 1 bank angle and the Cue Ball Line. This angle would require a 3/4 Full Left Hit to send the Object Ball onto the 2 to 1 path. Learn this angle well because it contains the key to one of the most reliable bank methods known to man.

The secret to locking down this common cross–table bank angle is to cut the Object Ball just a *hair* toward the 2 to 1 line instead of hitting dead full.

DO NOT cut the Object Ball back toward the 2 to 1 line. You only want to hit the Object Ball a millimeter to the side so the Cue Ball caroms a few inches toward the pocket. If you actually cut the Object Ball back toward the 2 to 1 line, it will land short

The Cue Ball only crosses one leg of the bank which is why I call these **Side–Step Banks**. The name also reminds me of the ball action needed to send the Object Ball dead into the pocket. A small "side–step" by the Cue Ball tells me that the Object Ball is getting the correct ball action to score.

SIDE–STEP Up And Back

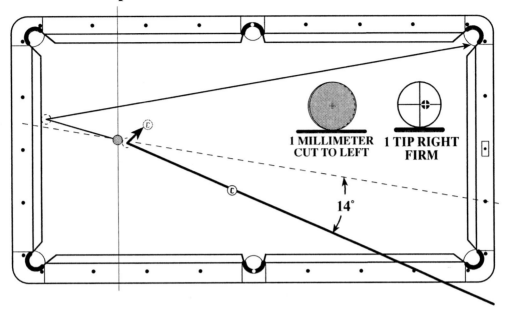

1 MILLIMETER CUT TO LEFT   **1 TIP RIGHT FIRM**

14°

When you hit a **Side–Step Bank** properly the Cue Ball only passes over the first leg of the bank angle a few inches. If the Object Ball lands short, you cut the ball too much and need to hit fuller. The cut on the Object Ball is *very small*. You only want to billiard the Cue Ball 3 or 4 inches toward the target pocket.

Old–time Straight–Rail players called these caroms "deadball billiards" because the nearly full hit on the Object Ball absorbs almost all of the force of the stroke leaving the Cue Ball with just enough energy to **Side–Step** a couple of inches. You only want the Cue Ball to *Passover* a couple of ball spaces.

Once you learn to identify the **Side–Step Bank** angle and begin playing for the position, your average on cross table banks will soar.

The **Side–Step Bank** is very reliable under pressure, which is why I like it so much. Once you get the hang of the shot, you will rarely miss a Side–Step Bank.

Side–Step Bank Action works equally well on Up and Back Banks or wherever it appears on the table. Cross–Sides, Cross–Corners and long angle shots all fall under the power of the mighty **Side–Step Bank**.   When you see the Side–Step angle, meaning that a 3/4 full hit would drive the Object Ball into the 2 to 1 path, you have one of the easiest banks to make.

SIDE–STEP ANGLE

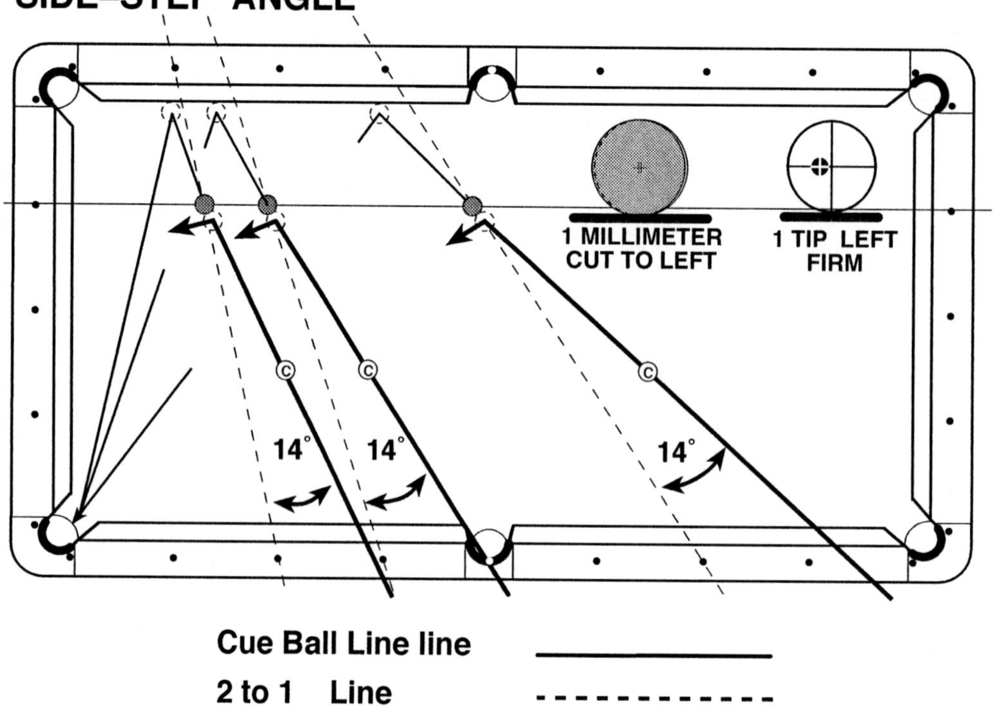

1 MILLIMETER CUT TO LEFT

1 TIP LEFT FIRM

14°   14°   14°

Cue Ball Line line   _____

2 to 1   Line   - - - - - - - - - - - -

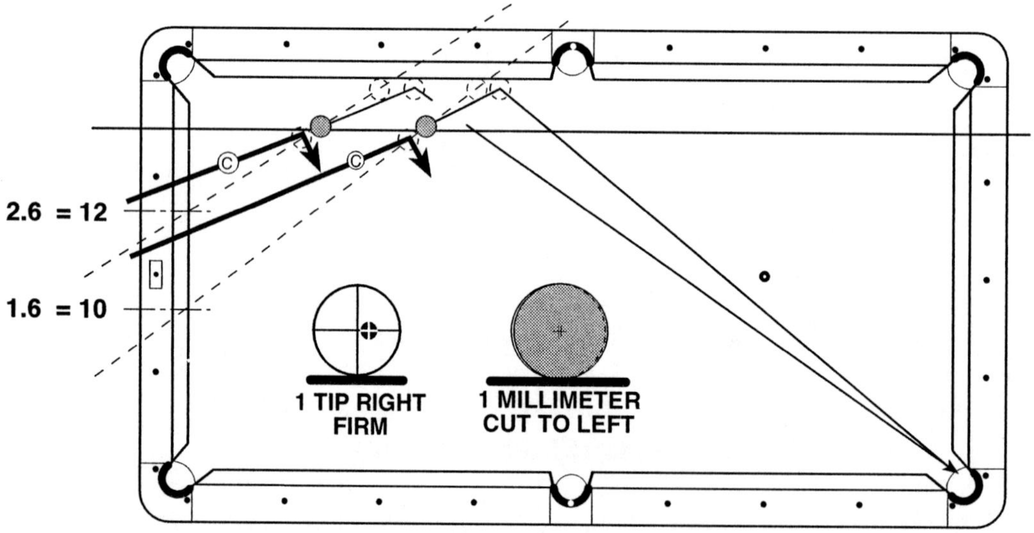

2.6 = 12

1.6 = 10

1 TIP RIGHT FIRM

1 MILLIMETER CUT TO LEFT

Set up **Side–Step Bank** positions and practice them until you engrave the 14° angle between the Cue Ball line and the Object Ball 2 to 1 line into your mind. Learn to recognize this bank angle whenever and wherever it pops up because with a little practice you will own this shot.

Once you begin playing the **Side–Step Bank** properly, your consistency on the shot will soar, no matter where it comes up.

When leaving a scary place with a big bankroll, put your money in at least three different pockets to foil a potential heist-man. Only a very experienced stick-up guy will ask you to empty more than two pockets. Put the big bills in the third pocket. Forget your shoes. Even a novice robber will make you take off your shoes.

Kilroy's Rules Of The Road

A good place to hide your bankroll in a motel room is inside the shower-curtain rod. It's hollow and can be easily removed and replaced.

You may have to remove 1 or 2 screws, so pack a combination, Phillips/Square-head screwdriver for such occasions.

Don't quote me on this, but a shower-curtain rod also makes a good stash for illicit chemicals.

Kilroy's Rules Of The Road

LONG CROSS BANKS

Here's a diagram showing the intersection points on the short rail for long cross–corner banks.

In order to figure long cross-banks we must mentally extend the table to 14 Diamonds. It is difficult to visualize these imaginary Diamond positions accurately, so a diagram is provided that geometrically shows the intersection points on the short rail.

These tracks are the starting point for aiming long cross-banks.

In a bit we'll learn what to do to make these banks, but the beginning is learning the extended bank paths.

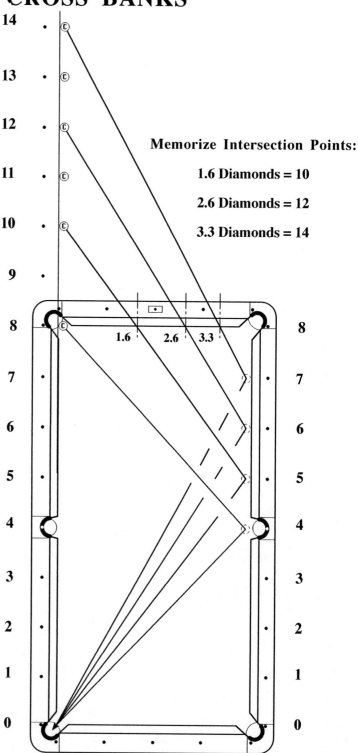

Memorize Intersection Points:

1.6 Diamonds = 10

2.6 Diamonds = 12

3.3 Diamonds = 14

LONG SIDE BANKS

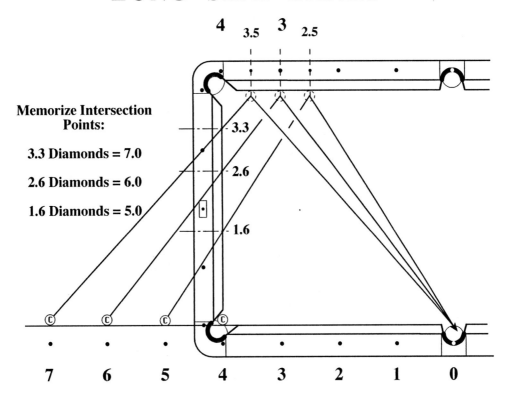

This diagram shows the intersection points on the short rail for side pocket banks that start beyond the long rail.

We could mentally extend the table 3 Diamonds past the short rail, but doing this geometrically and memorizing the intersection points on the short rail helps avoid confusion in competition.

Here again we do our calculations **OPPOSITE** the Diamond positions instead of aiming through the Diamonds.

Learning these bank tracks improves performance.

EXTENDED SHORT RAIL SYSTEM

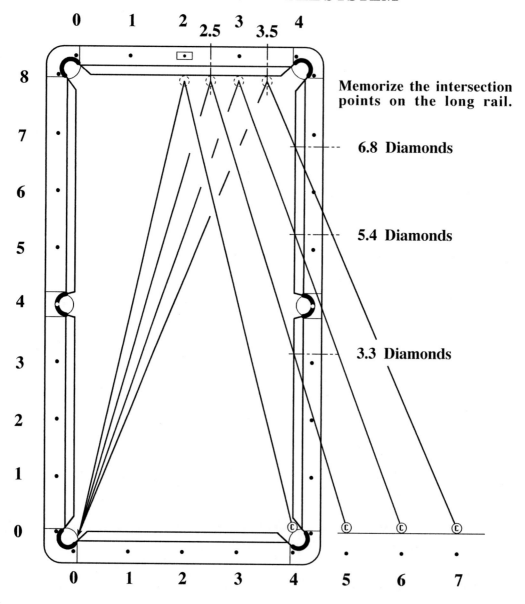

Memorize the intersection points on the long rail.

6.8 Diamonds

5.4 Diamonds

3.3 Diamonds

By extending imaginary Diamonds we can calculate banks with starting points beyond the end rails.

The bank paths shown are reference tracks and the proper ball action is needed to score.

"After this fellow banked the money ball in seven or eight times in a row, I began to get the feeling that *I* was the one being hustled."

Roadman **"Toledo Joe" Thomas** remarking on his first encounter with bank shot legend Eddie Taylor.

STANDARD BREAK

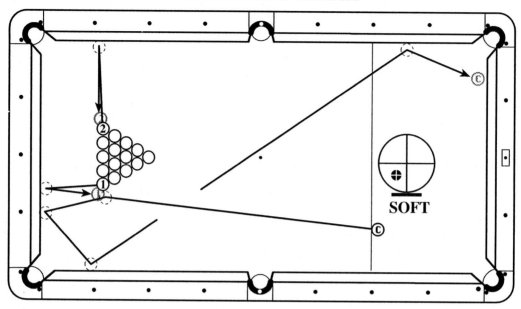

SOFT

Before explaining the break a question must be answered. Should you break the balls open or play safe. And if you play safe, how safe should you play.

I played with every champion and I know of no great banker, when playing for big money, who broke the balls wide open. Not one! That should answer the questions.

If you are playing for laughs or you just want to get in stroke, it's all right to smash the rack, but in tough competition you must break safe.

The break illustrated above and the one on the next page are the safe breaks I recommend learning.

The break above is the classic 14–1 Straight Pool break shot. Hit the 1-ball thin using two tips of low Outside English and spin the Cue Ball down to the end rail.

The ideal break shown above is seldom achieved. Usually the balls scatter a bit leaving possible, but very difficult shots.

MY FAVORITE BREAK SHOT

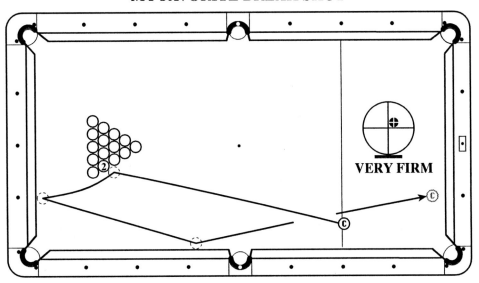

VERY FIRM

This is the break shot I use for bank pool. It's somewhat stronger because it opens up the balls a little more and also leaves your opponent stuck on the end rail. This break applies more pressure in case the opposition wants to take a swing at a straight back shot.

Use 1 Tip Right–Hand Follow and aim to hit the top of the 2–ball. Hit the shot pretty firm because the Reverse English slows the Cue Ball down coming back.

A GOOD RESULT

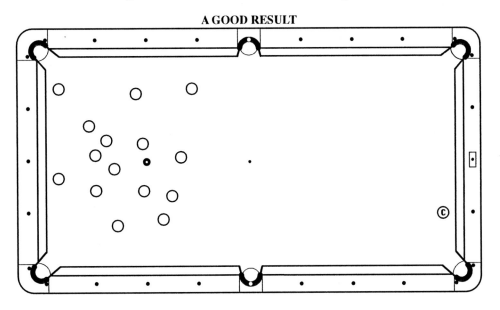

This is a strong break because your opponent has no shot and cannot return the Cue Ball to the Head Rail.

TWO RAIL BANK POOL SAFETY

Safety play in bank pool often contends with balls lined up behind the spot.

With at least four balls behind the spot, shoot 2–rails using 2 Tips of Right–Hand English with **Firm Speed**.

The Cue Ball spins off one of the middle balls (grey) and returns to the head rail for a safety.

The first cushion target for this shot is to hit opposite Diamond 1, which sends the Cue Ball toward the side pocket. (5.0 – 1.0 = 4.0)

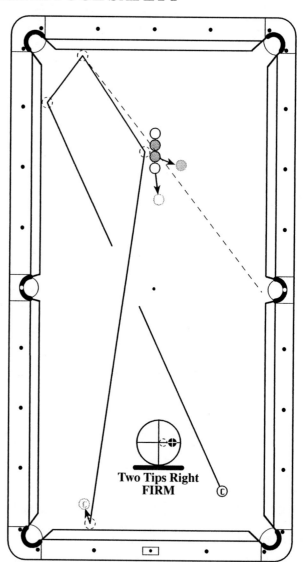

Two Tips Right
FIRM

ONE-RAIL BANK POOL SAFETY

This time the 2-rail safety is blocked, so we reply with a strong one-rail kick that leaves the opposition in a difficult situation.

Use 2 Tips of Left-Hand English, medium speed, and the Cue Ball spins off one of the middle balls (grey) and returns to the head rail for a safety.

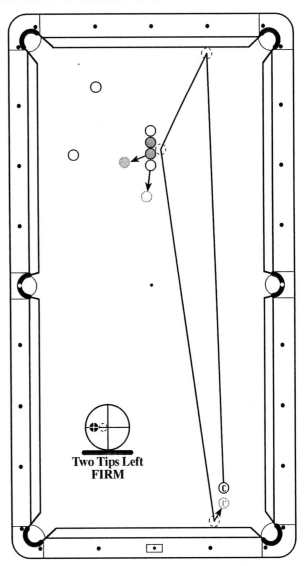

Two Tips Left
FIRM

STRATEGY

To counter safety play designed to slow the game up and meant to discourage aggressive shooting, you need to place at least **two** balls at the head of the table.

In the beginning of the game, look to put your opponent underneath a ball or balls at the foot of the table (where you rack the balls). By that I mean you should try to freeze him behind the main body of balls at the foot of the table. You want to keep the opposition from returning the Cue Ball to the back rail (head of the table).

When an opponent leaves you at the foot of the table your main job is to ignore any marginal shots you may have and instead shoot at least one ball to the head or end rail, and snooker your opponent to keep him from seeing, and then being able to move that ball back to the foot of the table.

If opponents are snookered they will not play a safety to the head rail because that would allow you to either have a shot at the ball that you previously put there, or you could shoot it away and leave him frozen on the back rail and far away from the body of balls.

Since you are going to be left at the foot of the table again, you ignore any marginal shots — your main objective is to get two balls up table by shooting a second ball up to the head of the table — completing your mission.

If that is not possible, play again to snooker your foe from seeing the balls on the head rail and force your opponent to leave you among the balls at the foot of the table again.

Once two balls are at the back end (head) of the table, refrain from shooting a marginal straight-back with any one of them. Because once you miss your opponent will remove the remaining ball there by either playing safe or playing a shot with it. In either case you will be back where you started. Better to find another ball to shoot to the head rail (as a move) to bring the count to three. The more balls at the head of the table the merrier.

Conversely, if you are the one trying to slow the game down, then you would naturally look to remove any single ball from the head of the table to keep two balls from collecting there.

End Game Strategy

At the end of game, if you are behind and want to put balls into play your initial objective is to get two balls on the foot spot and to leave your opponent on the head rail. Your opponent will seldom choose to play safe off spotted balls, because it is usually difficult to get the Cue Ball back to the head rail due to balls at the foot of the table that may be in the way. This allows you to shoot in more balls that will also be spotted, and pretty soon all or many of the balls will be in play.

On the other hand, when you are protecting a lead and a ball lands on the foot spot it is your job to remove it at once to keep others from collecting.

When you need one ball, your strategy should be to take at least one and possibly two balls out of play — hang a ball in one of the corner pockets at the foot of the table. This is much better than hanging balls in the corners at the head of the table as they can be readily shot in, re-spotted and put back into play. The balls hanging in the front corner pockets at the foot of the table are usually difficult to make without leaving a shot after they are spotted.

Key Point

Do not take *all* the balls out of play — a fatal mistake that I myself made for years — my rationale was, "If one ball out of play is good, then three or four is better still." A flawed conclusion it turns out.

If you and your opponent are both playing one ball at a time, you remove much of the pressure from your opponent. All the opposition has to do is play safe on one ball.

If there are several balls in play, even though they might present an opportunity for your opponent to make them in one inning, it also makes it many times more difficult for the opposition to play safe when you only need one ball. One ball could be made from anywhere. Your foe will be under extreme pressure trying to keep you from shooting at 2-rail or 3-rail banks that will win the game. Paranoia will have your competition seeing banks going in from everywhere.

Your opponent knows that any ball you are left close to, regardless of the angle, is a possible make. With one ball in play on the table, if the other player keeps leaving you long with the Cue Ball near the cushion, the pressure between the two of you would be about the same. Maybe less for him because he is behind and has nothing to lose. But when he looks at the table and negatively visualizes that he cannot leave you without a shot, and that he has to leave you something to shoot at, the pressure becomes greater on him than you.

THE BEARD'S BANK DRILL

Start with Cue Ball in hand and bank the 1–ball cross–corner.

Play position and bank the remaining balls in any order without touching any other ball.

Bank as many balls in a row as you can. All 15 is a perfect score.

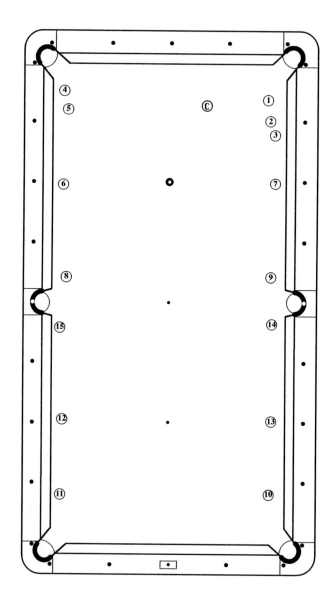

"Maximum throw is approximately one inch per foot."

BUD HARRIS, 3 Time US National 3 Cushion Champion.

AVOIDING KISSES

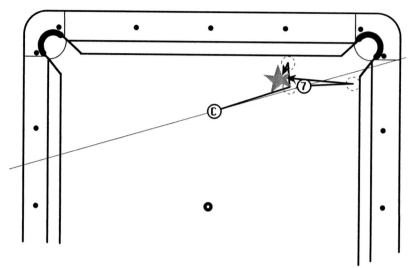

When the balls line up on a straight line to the middle of the **FACING** of the corner pocket, the bank is a dead kiss. It is extremely difficult to beat the kiss when the balls are on a line to the middle of the **FACING**.

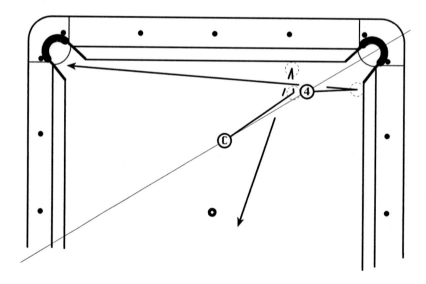

When the balls line up on a straight line to the **MIDDLE** of the **POCKET**, there is no kiss.

AVOIDING KISSES

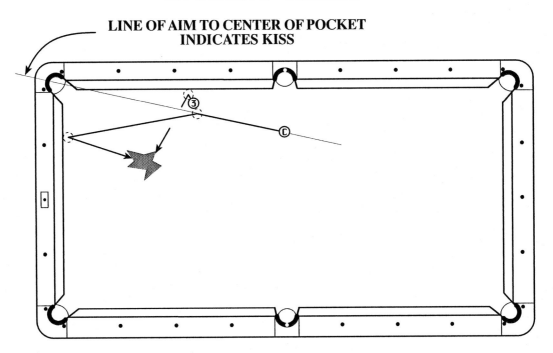

**LINE OF AIM TO CENTER OF POCKET
INDICATES KISS**

When the Cue Ball and an imaginary ball at the contact point for the bank are on a line to the center of the pocket, there is a dead kiss if you use follow with no english.

These kisses are usually easy to evade by using english or draw to send the Cue Ball on a non-kiss path.

The aim on the Object Ball must be adjusted to allow for the ball action needed for a non–kiss bank.

CLOTH EFFECTS

The cloth is put on a table with the *nap*, or *threads* or *grain* of the cloth, running between the end or short rails.   The cloth should be installed with the grain running *toward* the *foot* of the table (where you rack the balls).   This end of the table is known (especially to Three Cushion billiard players) as the **long end** of the table.

Long end and **short end**, are billiard terms, and refer to the fact that a ball rolling slowly toward the corner coming off the long rail rolls *long* to the short rail on the **long end** and *short* toward the long rail on the **short end.**

When a ball rolls toward the **long end** of the table, you are going *with* the grain of the cloth.   Conversely, a ball rolling toward the *head* of the table will be going *against* the grain and toward the **short end** of the table.

A ball traveling *with* the grain moves slightly faster than when it rolls *against* the grain.

A ball rolling between the side rails slows up quicker than it would between the end rails because it is running *across* the grain or nap.   That is why balls tend to freeze to the long rails more so than to the short rails.   Think of the ball going bump-bump across the railroad tracks and the last track then hampering the ball from coming unfrozen and locking the ball into the rail.

Every English Snooker player knows, but few American players are aware, that Cue Balls hit easy with english will keep hooking in the direction that the spin is applied when the Cue Ball is shot slowly against the grain toward the **short end**.

Conversely, a Cue Ball hit at easy speed toward the **long end**, with the grain, will lose its hook or curve, and straighten out and begin to go toward the **end rail**. You can keep the Cue Ball hooking in the direction of the applied english when shooting toward the **long end**, provided you use a little more speed and stroke. Over-stroking can carry the hook all the way down the table on the **long end**; it's just much easier to do it on the **short end**.   The stroke and how long the tip stays on the Cue Ball determines how long you can keep the spin on the ball and thereby defy the resistance of the cloth.   However, remember that once the applied *torque* on the stroke wears off, the ball will turn in the opposite direction on the **long end**. Shots hit easy will have to be aimed with the resistance or non-resistance of the cloth included in the shot calculations.

These allowances are a factor to be considered even with so-called, "non-directional" cloth.

There are several easy ways to immediately determine the **long** and **short end** of any table. Probably the simplest test is to shoot the Cue Ball out of the corner three rails to the opposite corner. Shooting out of a corner, aim at approximately 2-1/2 diamonds on the first-rail with favoring english. Shoot the same shot out of all four corners and note the results. Coming slowly off the third rail, you will notice that the ball will begin to favor rolling to either the end rail or the side rail. If the ball favors or tilts toward the **long rail** that is the **short end** of the table. If the ball begins to seek the **short** or **end rail**, that will be the **long end** of the table.

All of this presumes that the table is relatively level.

New Cloth, Slightly Used Cloth and Old Cloth (no nap)

New Cloth: Cut Bank hit easy — the Object Ball "curls" off cushion in the direction of the pocket. The smooth new nap keeps the curl on longer, resulting in balls breaking very long.

Slightly Used Cloth: Cut Bank hit easy — the Object Ball also "curls" off cushion in the direction of the pocket. The slightly used nap retains curl somewhat, but ball doesn't break as long as it does with new cloth.

Old Cloth, no-nap (very worn): Cut Bank hit easy — the Object Ball "curls" off cushion in the direction of the pocket, but the worn, rough, "no-nap" creates more friction and burns up curl quickly. The ball quickly straightens out and stops breaking.

New Cloth: Passover Bank hit easy — the Object Ball "curls" off cushion in the direction of the pocket. The collision-induced english also turns the ball in that same direction. The smooth nap retains curl and collision-induced english, and the ball breaks very long.

Slightly Used Cloth: Passover Bank hit easy — the Object Ball "curls" off cushion in the direction of the pocket. The collision-induced english also turns the ball in that same direction. The thinner nap doesn't retain curl and collision-induced english, and the ball doesn't break as long as with new cloth.

Old Cloth (no nap): Passover Bank hit easy — the Object Ball "curls" off cushion in the direction of the pocket. The **Collision-Induced-English** also turns the ball in that same direction. The rough, no-nap burns up curl and collision-induced english quickly, and the ball stops breaking and straightens out quickly.

Cushion Effects: The amount of **Collision-Induced-Throw** and *Acquired English* is directly proportionate to the distance the Object Ball is from the cushion and the amount of pressure that the Object Ball applies to the cushion.

The more penetration by an Object Ball that is *shot* into a cushion with no Cue Ball applied english, results in the Object Ball running **longer** than the natural angle (a *Cue Ball* shot directly into a cushion by a cue stick will give differing results because the Cue Ball is being propelled and acted upon by a cue tip). Naturally penetration is determined by the speed of the Object Ball contacting the cushion. Lesser penetration of the Object Ball will shorten the angle.

However, when an Object Ball has been infected with Cue Ball applied english, a different thing entirely occurs. The more penetration into the cushion, the smaller the amount of english that "takes." Conversely, the least penetration will result in the most english working off the cushion.

You can get the deepest penetration when the Object Ball is the closest to the cushion. You also don't need to hit a bank as hard if the ball is close to the cushion. When you bank a ball into the cushion and the ball is a diamond or more away from the rail, if you were playing a Cut Bank you would have to compensate considerably for the **Collision-Induced-Reverse-English** that would be in full bloom by the time it reaches the cushion. However, if the Object Ball was a long distance away from the cushion and was hit easily, the **Collision-Induced-English** may be worn off by friction before it contacts a cushion.

The curves that occur after the rebound can be seen if you stand near the table and watch the rebound path and the shot is not hit too hard.

NEW CLOTH

Think of the threads in the cloth as railroad tracks running from the Head Rail to the Foot Rail. Any ball running in these tracks will move faster. A ball will move even faster going with the grain (toward the foot of the table).

A ball rolling across the "railroad tracks" can be imagined as bumping over the "rails" as it rolls from one side rail to the other. A ball will therefore roll slower between the side rails on new or broken-in cloth. This is the reason balls freeze to the long rails more readily than the short rails. Think of railroad tracks "pinning" the ball to the cushion.

WORN-OUT CLOTH

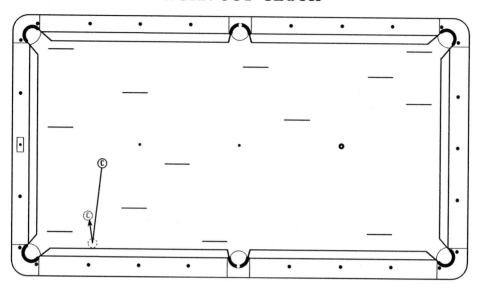

On worn-out cloth the threads are worn down and the nap is non-existent. The tracks between the end rails are gone and balls roll much slower going from the Head to the Foot of the table. With the tracks gone balls rolling between the long rails travel faster than a ball going from the Head to the Foot of the table.

Balls are less likely to freeze to the long rails on worn cloth.

PATH DEVIATION

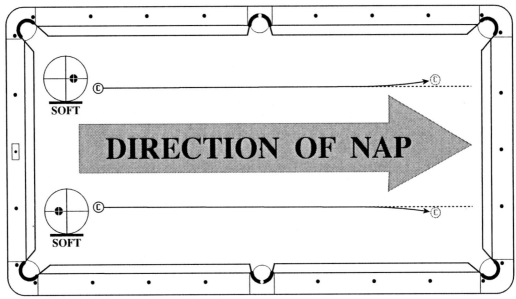

CURVES EXAGGERATED FOR CLARITY

During the last inches of its journey a slowly rolling Cue Ball will veer slightly to the side opposite the english applied to the ball. This is to say that the Cue Ball will veer slightly to the left when hit with right–hand english.

Conversely, a ball hit with Left-English will veer slightly to the right when the english wears off.

Contrariwise, when you shoot against the grain toward the head of the table the effects are reversed. This is to say, Left-English breaks left and Right-English breaks right when going toward the head or short end of the table.

CLOTH EFFECTS

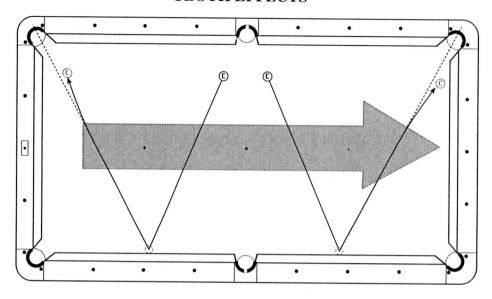

Due to cloth effects softly hit banks break slightly in the indicated directions.

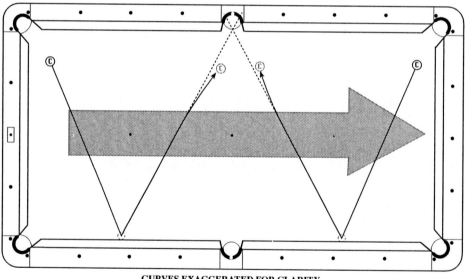

CURVES EXAGGERATED FOR CLARITY

CLOTH EFFECTS

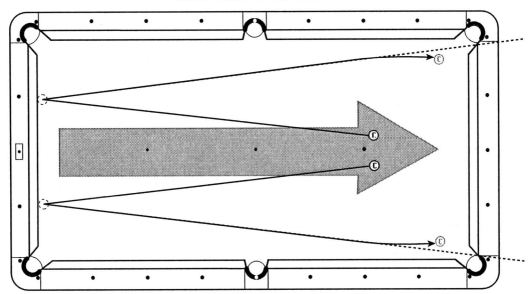

Banks going toward Foot of the table roll long.

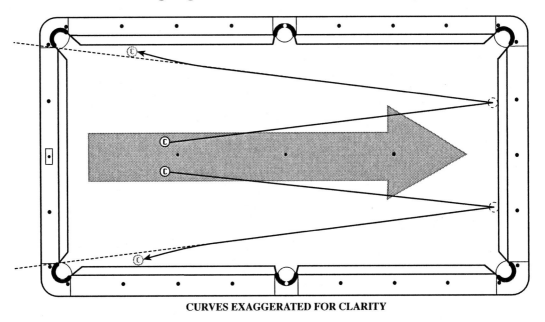

CURVES EXAGGERATED FOR CLARITY

Banks to the Head of the table roll short.

CLOTH EFFECTS

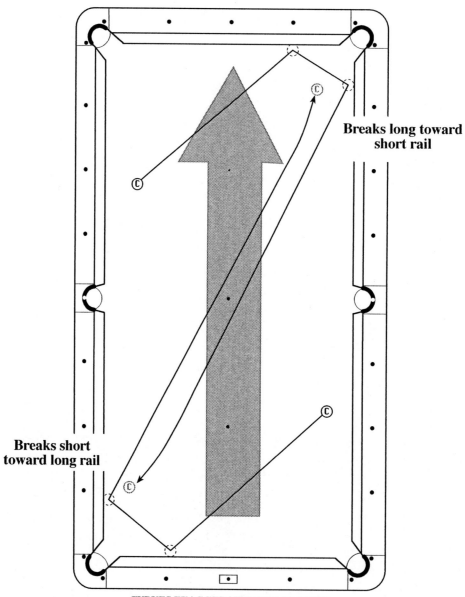

Breaks long toward
short rail

Breaks short
toward long rail

CURVES EXAGGERATED FOR CLARITY

CLOTH EFFECTS

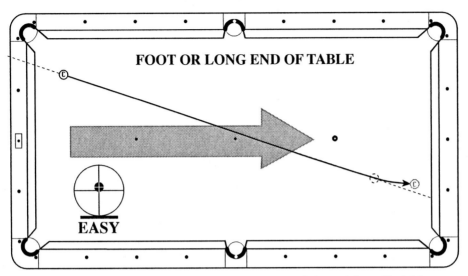

A softly hit Cue Ball going toward the foot of the table will drift away from the pocket at the end of its journey.

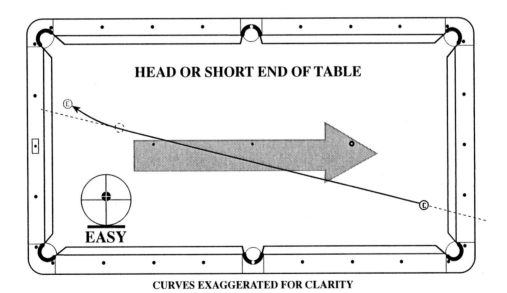

A softly hit Cue Ball shot to the head of the table will drift toward the pocket at the end of its journey.

FOOT OR LONG END OF TABLE

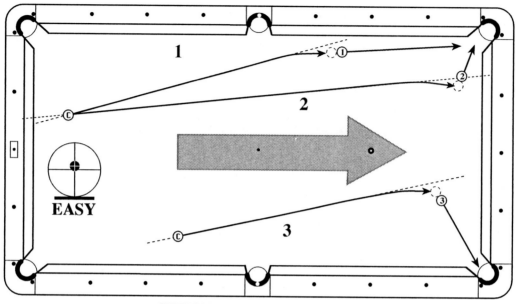

CURVES EXAGGERATED FOR CLARITY

SHOT 1

Because of the nap of the cloth, on a slowly hit ball you must aim to cut the Object Ball thinner. The direction of the threads of the cloth pulls the Cue Ball off its original path, and the Cue Ball runs slightly long of its original path.

SHOT 2

Since we know the Cue Ball will deviate and run a bit long on an easy hit, the aim must be adjusted. Now we aim to hit the Object Ball slightly fuller. At the end of its journey, the Cue Ball will turn slightly away from the Object Ball helping the Cut Angle.

SHOT 3

The same cloth effects already explained turn the Cue Ball a little at the end of its roll, requiring a thinner aim to score.

NOTE: The actual adjustment needed for these shots is 1/8 to 1/4 Ball, more or less, depending on the direction of the shot.

Although the corrections are small, they are critical for making these shots.

HEAD OR SHORT END OF TABLE

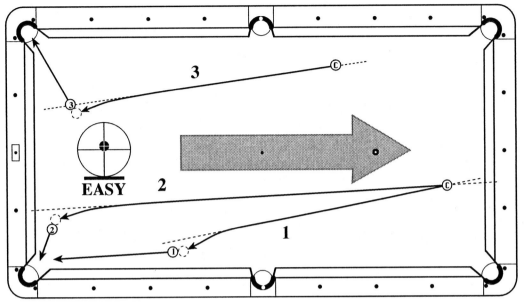

CURVES EXAGGERATED FOR CLARITY

SHOT 1

When we shoot toward the Head, or Short End of the table, everything is reversed.

We must aim to cut the Object Ball less. The direction of the threads of the cloth pulls the Cue Ball off its original path, and the Cue Ball runs slightly short of its original path.

SHOT 2

With Easy Speed the Cue Ball deviate and runs a bit short toward the Head of the Table, Now we aim to hit the Object Ball slightly thinner. At the end of its journey, the Cue Ball will turn slightly toward the Object Ball, helping get the fuller hit needed to score.

SHOT 3

The same cloth effects turn the Cue Ball a little short, needing a slightly fuller aim to score.

NOTE: The actual adjustment needed for these shots is 1/8 to 1/4 Ball Space, more or less, depending on the direction of the shot.

CLOTH EFFECTS

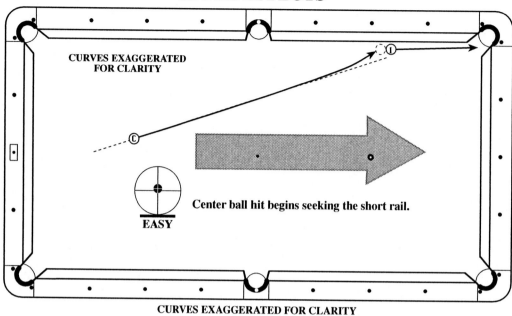

CURVES EXAGGERATED
FOR CLARITY

Center ball hit begins seeking the short rail.

EASY

CURVES EXAGGERATED FOR CLARITY

A Cue Ball shot toward the long end turns into the Object Ball, and under-cuts it at the end of its path as it begins to seek the short rail.

The solution is to use one tip of reverse english (inside english). Use right–hand english which turns the Cue Ball slightly to the left for a proper hit to score.

These curves cause a deviation between 1/8 and 1/4 ball space.

In a game where millimeters make the difference between a champion and an also–ran, these small deviations in ball path are important for advanced play.

HEAD OR SHORT END OF TABLE

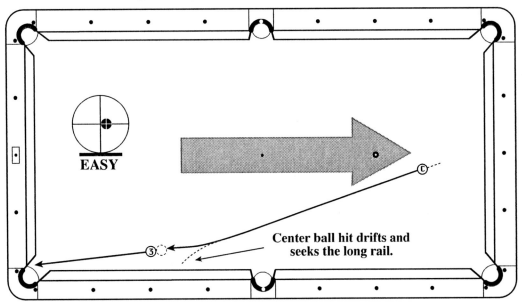

EASY

Center ball hit drifts and
seeks the long rail.

CURVES EXAGGERATED FOR CLARITY

A Cue Ball shot toward the short end turns away from the Object Ball, and over-cuts it at the end of its path as it begins to seek the long rail.

The solution is to use one tip of reverse english (inside english). Use right–hand english, which turns the Cue Ball slightly to the right for a proper hit to score.

These curves cause a deviation between 1/8 and 1/4 ball space. The curves are exaggerated in the illustrations for clarity.

BUNT SPEED

When a ball is hit **VERY EASY** with no english and is at least 2 diamonds away from the pocket, the Object Ball will first slide a few inches, then convert to rolling ball and roll end over end on a direct path to the pocket.

If the ball has to travel a long way (over 4 diamonds) the Object Ball will be subject to the effects of the nap of the cloth that alter its path. Most of these effects are described in the Cloth and Cushion diagrams.

BUNT SPEED SHOT

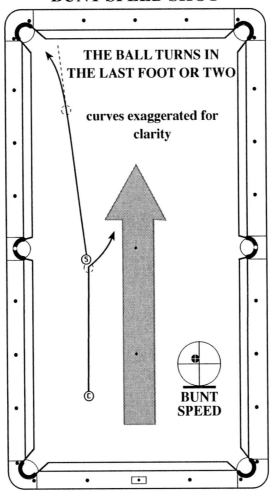

THE BALL TURNS IN THE LAST FOOT OR TWO

curves exaggerated for clarity

BUNT SPEED

On a long, softly hit shot that barely makes it to the pocket (as you might do in One–Pocket), if you use 1 Tip of Inside Follow english at a very slow speed, the Object Ball will begin to turn in the direction of the applied english at the end of its path.

Please Note: The curves we are considering are small, only changing the path of the Object Ball 1/8 to 1/4 Ball Space. Nonetheless, allowing for these curves is critical in high speed One-Pocket.

BUNT SPEED SHOT

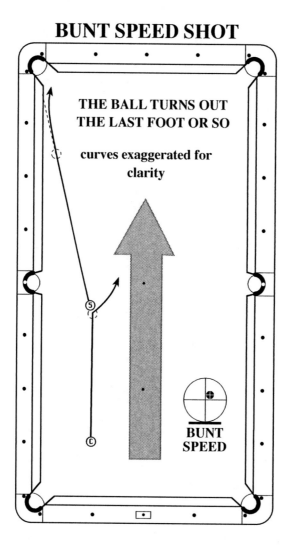

THE BALL TURNS OUT THE LAST FOOT OR SO

curves exaggerated for clarity

BUNT
SPEED

On the same shot, using 1 Tip of Outside Follow english at a very slow speed, the Object Ball will begin to turn in the direction of the applied english at the end of its path.

BUNT SPEED SHOT

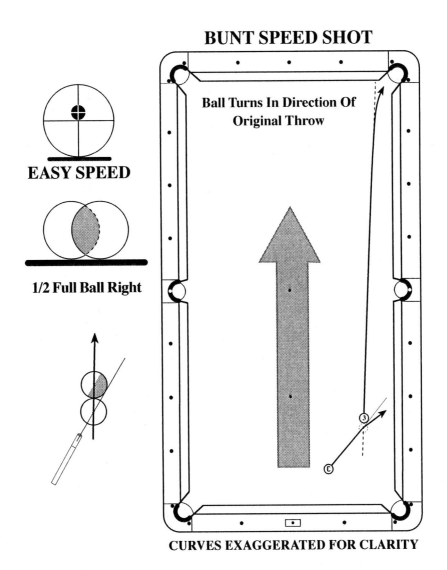

EASY SPEED

1/2 Full Ball Right

Ball Turns In Direction Of Original Throw

CURVES EXAGGERATED FOR CLARITY

Very Easy Speed, 1 Tip Follow, No English.

With 1/2 ball or thinner cut, the **Collision-Induced-Throw** kicks in at the end of the ball's path and turns slightly in the direction of the cut.

Cut Bank

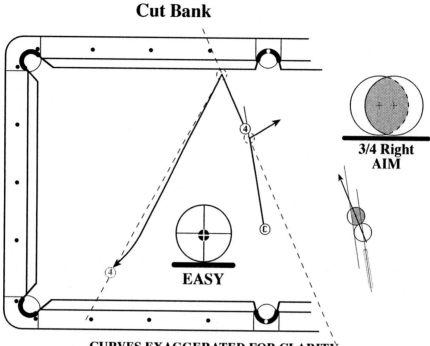

3/4 Right AIM

EASY

CURVES EXAGGERATED FOR CLARITY

Collision-Induced Reverse English causes the Object Ball to break away from the pocket, but when the english wears off, the ball stops breaking and veers slightly toward the pocket.

Passover Bank

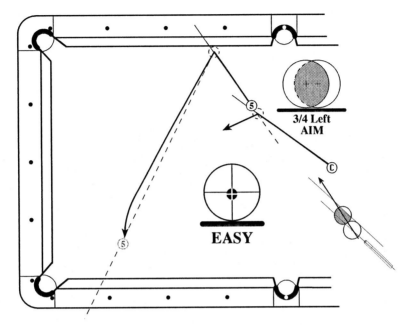

3/4 Left AIM

EASY

CURVES EXAGGERATED FOR CLARITY

Collision-Induced Running English causes the Object Ball to break toward the pocket, but when the english wears off, the Object Ball stops breaking and veers slightly away from the pocket.

EFFECTS OF SPEED

HARD SPEED

Hard — Kills (reduces) the effects of **Follow, Draw** and **English.**

Hard — Cuts the ball OK because speed erases most **Collision–Induced–Throw.** This is based on the billiard principle that "Speed Kills Action."

Here's something else about **Hard Speed.** If you are trying to put english on the Object Ball and you shoot **Hard,** the english will barely affect the Object Ball. About 50% of the english effect is lost with **Hard Speed.** This is also based on the "Speed Kills Action" principle.

More accurately, and this is for the *purists*, the linear force generated by **Hard Speed** overrules the rotational energy provided by english or Cut Angle. Speed **reduces** and **delays** the effects of ball action. If enough force is used, the effects of ball action are reduced to insignificance or delayed until the shot is finished.

We can also simply say "Speed Kills Action."

Hard — It *is* possible to get **Follow, Draw** and **English** to work with **Hard Speed** but you need a super stroke to impart the necessary amount of top and bottom spin. You need to apply at least **2 Tips Of English** to get **One Tip** to work, because you lose approximately 50% of the english effect on the Object Ball using **Hard Speed.** In practical play we seldom use extreme english. Such shots are usually reserved for the trick shot exhibitions. Ninety-five percent of the shots we need to shoot do not require drastic measures.

FIRM SPEED

Firm — Runs 1/4 Diamond short on Straight-On and Cut Angle Banks

Firm — Aim on the money on Passover Angles

Firm — **Draw** lengthens bank angles 1/4 Diamond.

Firm — **1 Tip English** changes the bank angle 1/4 Diamond

Firm — **Follow** shortens bank angle 1/4 Diamond

EFFECTS OF SPEED

EASY SPEED

Easy — On the mark for Natural or Cut Angle Banks

Easy — 1/4 Diamond long for Passover Banks

Easy — **2 Tips English** lengthens bank angle 1/4 Diamond

Easy — About 50% of the english effect is lost with **Easy Speed**

Cut Banks

Hard — Aim right at the point of a "divide the angle" aim.

Firm — 1/4 ball more cut (thinner, because it falls short of natural angle)

Easy — Aim right at the point of a "divide the angle" aim.

Passover Banks

Hard — 1/4 ball more cut than natural angle (aim thinner)

Firm — Aim on the "divide the angle" path (the natural angle will score)

PLUS AND MINUS CHART

Cut Banks

Minus 1	—	*shortens every Cut Bank 1/4 diamond*
Minus 2	—	*shortens every Cut Bank 1/2 diamond*
Zero	—	*at 0 the bank scores*
Plus 1	—	*lengthens every Cut Bank 1/4 diamond*
Plus 2	—	*lengthens every Cut Bank 1/2 diamond*

Natural Divide The Angle Cut Bank	=	minus 1
Firm Follow	=	minus 1 *(when **Follow** "works," it shortens angle)*
Firm center ball (stop) hit	=	minus 1
Easy center ball (stop) hit	=	minus 1 *(using just enough speed to stop the Cue Ball)*

1 tip of Firm	inside *(**Reverse**)* english	=	minus 1
2 tips of Hard	inside *(**Reverse**)* english	=	minus 1
2 tips of Easy	inside *(**Reverse**)* english	=	minus 1
2 tips of Firm	inside *(**Reverse**)* english	=	minus 2

Hard Follow	=	0 change
Hard Draw	=	plus 1 *(only **Hard Draw** works)*
Subtracting 1/4 diamond (aim closer to pocket)	=	plus 1
Easy	=	plus 1
Easy Draw	=	plus 1 *(most **Draw** effect used up by cloth friction)*

2 Tips Firm Draw		=	plus 1
1 tip Firm	outside *(**Opposite**)* english	=	plus 1
2 tips of Hard	outside *(**Opposite**)* english	=	plus 1
2 tips of Easy	outside *(**Opposite**)* english	=	plus 1
2 tips of Firm	outside *(**Opposite**)* english	=	plus 2
1 tip of Easy	outside *(**Opposite**)* english	=	0 english effect on cushion
1 tip of Easy	outside *(**Opposite**)* english	=	about 1/8 diamond of Object Ball Throw
1 tip of Hard	outside *(**Opposite**)* english	=	0 english effect on cushion
1 tip of Hard	outside *(**Opposite**)* english	=	about 1/8 diamond of Object Ball Throw

PLUS AND MINUS CHART

Cut Banks   continued

1 tip of Easy	inside (**Reverse**) english	=	0 english effect on cushion
1 tip of Easy	inside (**Reverse**) english	=	about 1/8 diamond of Object Ball throw
1 tip of Hard	inside (**Reverse**) english	=	0 english effect on cushion
1 tip of Hard	inside (**Reverse**) english	=	about 1/8 diamond of Object Ball throw

PLUS AND MINUS CHART

Passover Banks

Minus 1	=	*shortens bank 1/4 diamond*
Minus 2	=	*shortens bank 1/2 diamond*
Zero	=	*at 0 the bank scores*
Plus 1	=	*lengthens bank 1/4 diamond*
Plus 2	=	*lengthens bank 1/2 diamond*

Natural Divide The Angle	=	0
Aim 1/4 ball fuller (subtract 1/4 diamond from the angle)	=	plus 1
Hard Follow	=	0 (only hard speed works)
Hard Draw	=	0 (only hard speed works)
Hard Center (1/2 tip above or below center)	=	plus 1
Firm Follow (2 tips)	=	minus 1 (runs short)
Firm Draw (2 tips)	=	plus 1
Firm center (1/2 tip above or below center)	=	0
Easy Follow (Object Ball rolling naturally)	=	plus 1 (follow effect wears off before it contacts cushion)
Easy Draw	=	plus 1 (most draw effect used up by cloth friction)
2 tips of Hard (outside) Reverse english	=	minus 1
1 tip of Hard (outside) Reverse english	=	0
2 tips of Firm (outside) Reverse english	=	minus 2
1 tip of Firm (outside) Reverse english	=	minus 1
2 tips of easy (outside) Reverse english	=	minus 1
1 tip of easy (outside) Reverse english	=	0 (actually shortens about 1/8th diamond)
2 tips of Hard (inside) Running english	=	plus 1
1 tip of Hard (inside) Running english	=	0

PLUS AND MINUS CHART

Passover Banks   **continued**

2 tips of Firm (inside) Running english	=	plus 2
1 tip of Firm (inside) Running english	=	plus 1
2 tips of easy (inside) Running english	=	plus 1
1 tip of easy (inside) Running english	=	0 (actually lengthens about 1/8th diamond)

AIMING WITH ENGLISH

Aim using english the same as you would with a center ball hit on the Cue Ball.

If you mentally parallel another Cue Stick from the english side of the Cue Stick toward the center of the Cue Ball, the center ball line up should be the same as the normal aim without english.

ADJUSTING FOR DISTANCE

The toughest part of this lesson is making the adjustments for distance. You must keep in mind that this system depends on the Object Ball having the necessary speed and english **when it contacts the rail**. Everything that happens in banks is determined by what the Object Ball is doing at the instant of contact with the cushion.

For example, a straight back bank with the Object Ball a long way from the cushion may have to be hit **Hard** to have **Firm** Speed effects when it contacts the cushion.

Conversely, when the Object Ball is close to the cushion and the Cue Ball is near to the Object Ball it is difficult to get Easy speed effect because of the short distance. There is not enough room for friction to do its work.

Adjustments will come through practice and experience.

ENGLISH FOR NON–BANK SHOTS

Basic Principle A — 1 Tip Of English applied with a Firm stroke will affect the Object Ball approximately the same as 1/4 Ball of cut.

Basic Principle B — You lose one tip of english shooting Hard or Easy. The Hard Speed "kills" the side-spin effect. Easy Speed loses the ball action before it gets to the cushion.

Favoring English — 1 Tip of Firm "favoring" english Requires 1/4 Ball less cut (fuller hit).

Reverse English — 1 Tip of Firm "Reverse" english Requires 1/4 Ball more cut (thinner hit).

WE'VE TAKEN POOL AND BILLIARDS OUT OF THE POOLHALL

You've never seen anything like this. No sweators. No dirt. No noise. Just pool and billiards on some of the finest equipment anywhere. And lessons available from world class players. Refreshments of course. Open from 10 a.m. Members only. Fifty dollars annual dues.

NORTH SHORE BILLIARD CLUB
2865 N. CLARK CHICAGO, ILL. 60614
312-472-2400

ARTIE BODENDORFER

Artie Bodendorfer, Chicago, IL, a great unknown player.

Artie was a tremendous percentage shooter. After playing with him for 24 hours, nobody had a chance. He could rob anybody after a day of play. His percentage shooting would then really start to matter. Plus, he could play for 2 or 3 days on coffee only, no pills, no food, and he never sat down. He would pee about once every 24 hours. Playing against him was so brutal that Artie had two people drop dead playing him. Both players succumbed to heart attacks while shooting at the game ball. One was Chicago's legendary, **Isadore "Pony" Rosen**.

Artie did not have a fancy stroke, but he was one of the greatest when it came to shooting off the game ball. His face, on the *cheese* shot, would look like somebody was squeezing his privates with a pair of pliers. Then Bodendorfer would uncork his straight-through, "jerk" stroke, and the *big-money* ball would drizzle into the pocket.

Bodendorfer gave out ridiculous handicaps to suckers, and even the best players found him next to impossible to beat, as several Hall of Fame members and a number of World Champions who dared cross cues with him discovered. However, I must add a footnote. Ninety-eight percent of Artie's wins came on his home court, Bensingers Billiard Academy.

Bensingers was located in a damp basement and was a very difficult place for anyone to win in. The air had such a low oxygen content that even the *short-stops* who played there had batting averages of eighty percent. Road players usually avoided the place as if they might catch malaria down there. In reality, the place was dark, dank, dirty, and smelly; and malaria may have been a possibility.

Artie was not without fault. He liked to get drunk and spit on barmaids. I personally witnessed the following scene — Artie was so obnoxiously drunk that two cops in a Paddy Wagon refused to arrest him because they had already experienced that nauseating pleasure once before. Artie dared them to arrest him! He was loudly cursing them out, hanging on to them, and slobbering on them, as the cops attempted to make their getaway. One of the cops climbed in the wagon, put his foot on Artie's chest, and shoved him out into the street. Then he promptly slammed the door, and the Paddy Wagon sped off into the night, leaving Artie behind, drooling, cursing, and sputtering.

Artie is the only pool player I know to have an airline make a special stop, on a nonstop flight, to heave him off the plane because he was so drunk and obnoxious.

EDDIE TAYLOR'S PROPOSITION BET

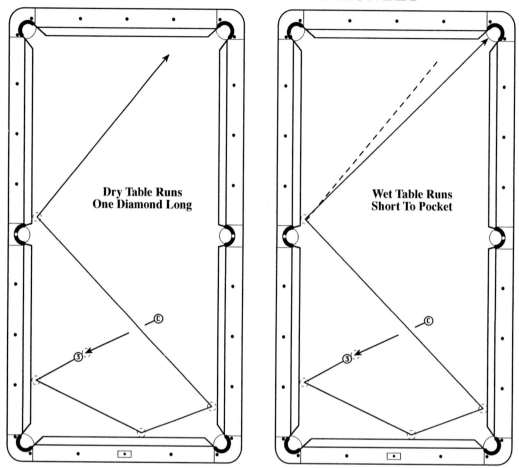

At the legendary Johnston City, Illinois Pool Jamboree back in the early 60s, I was privy to a bank-pool lesson from the master, **Eddie "The Knoxville Bear" Taylor**.

Bill "Weenie-Beanie" Staton, Larry "Boston Shorty" Johnson, Marshall "Squirrel" Carpenter and a few other top players were attempting a four rail One-Pocket bank shot with zero success. In spite of a good deal of kibbitzing, theorizing and experimentation, they were completely frustrated by the shot.

None of the approaches they tried worked. They hit the shot hard, they hit the shot easy, but the ball kept landing about a diamond long. They used every kind of english and stroke technique they could think of, but no one could shorten the shot that one little diamond.

They finally gave up and decided the shot couldn't be made, period.

At this point, Eddie Taylor (who suggested the shot to begin with) interjected that he could make the shot for a $500 bet. Even with Taylor's frightening reputation everyone figured the shot couldn't be made without a trick of some kind.

After Taylor assured everyone that he would make a legitimate bank, he got a play from millionaire "Weenie-Beanie," who said, "If he can make this, it'll be worth $500 just to learn how to shoot it!"

The money was put up and Taylor told someone to open the outside door near the table and said that he would shoot the shot in a few minutes. It was an arctic cold October day and the wind howled through the door giving everyone a shiver and bringing in much moisture and chill that was absorbed by the cushions. A few minutes later, Taylor had them close the door. Then he set up the shot and amazed everyone by drilling the bank in on the first try.

A few years later, I figured out what Eddie Taylor had done after a similar move got me broke at the Le Cue Club in Houston, Texas.

I was banking like a demon then and was even cocky enough to spot **Greg Stevens** a ball playing banks. We played my nine to his eight.

At that time Greg Stevens was an absolute pool monster. He handed out ridiculous spots to everybody playing nine-ball. Anyone could get the 6,7,8 and 9 if Stevens took the break. His shooting was legendary, as was his constitution. Stevens regularly stayed up playing pool for days at a time.

Greg kept the most phenomenal schedule I have ever seen. He would sleep for three days — Monday through Wednesday — then he would get up and eat. He would eat enough for the next four days, because that was how long he was going to stay up and play pool.

I ate with him only once. It was hideous. Stevens was like a pig in a trough. He ate at a 100 miles an hour and he ate everything in sight. In the space of half an hour Stevens packed away five or six big meals. He was the only guy I ever saw eat a whole loaf of Wonder Bread with a meal. Stevens would stay on his schedule of three days off and four days on with one meal in between for months at a time.

Stevens kept to this timetable for several years. After eating one gigantic meal Thursday, Greg wouldn't put anything else into his body for the next four days but coffee, cigarette smoke and speed pills. But, boy, he could really play. He might not miss 4 balls in 4 days.

However, Stevens didn't play bank pool like he played the other games, and this particular night I was pounding on him, raining 4's and 5's and getting out in 2, 3, or 4 innings every game. Then, suddenly, the banks started hanging up or coming short off the rail. Pretty soon I couldn't make anything and I fell dead.

You didn't want to fall dead in front of Greg, because he is a natural killer, and sure enough, with the help of the one ball spot, he turned things around and eventually broke me.

I was dumbfounded until an old "pool room detective" eased up and snitched off what had happened. "They turned off the air-conditioner on ya', boy. Them rails got soaked with moisture and you didn't adjust. Greg had 'em do it to slow you down. Seems like it worked just fine."

Then, I remembered Eddie Taylor and the shot he made in Johnston City. I now know moisture will liven up a cushion, and the balls will not penetrate the cushion as much and rebound faster and shorter. To make things more confusing the same moisture affects the cloth differently. While humidity speeds up the rebound off the cushion, the speed of the ball across the moisture-laden cloth is considerably slower, so damp rails play fast and short, and the cloth plays slower. Wet cloth also makes a table play tougher. Balls will hang up in the pockets, where on a dry cloth, the ball will slide cleanly into the pocket.

Those Texas boys got me by shutting the air-conditioner off, shortening all the angles, toughening up the pockets and confusing me to no end. I was too pool-ignorant at the time to adjust.

———————————●———————————

While I was being educated to the effects of air conditioning on bank shots, **Minnesota Fats (Rudolf Wanderone)** was also hanging out in the Le Cue playing regularly with **John "Lefty" Chapman**, one of the great black players of all time.

Chapman earned the additional nickname, **"Cannonball,"** while at the Le Cue. The name came from the monster Nine-Ball break Chapman had. Chapman was using a 26-oz break-cue, and his prodigious break sounded like a cannonball barreling through the rack.

An old road player named Ray Booth who was in Houston at the time described Chapman's break best. Booth said when his time was up and he was ready to go (die), he wanted to put his head on the foot spot and let "Cannonball" break the balls.

CANNONBALL LEFTY'S EVEN MONEY 3 RAIL BANK

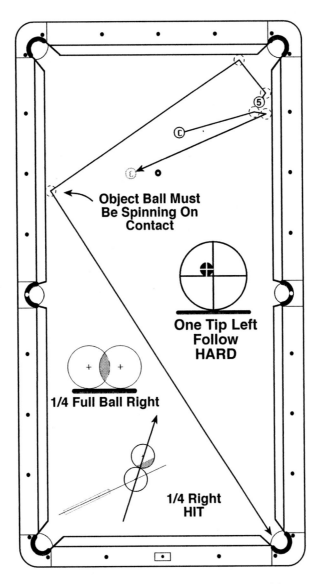

Lefty would bet his bankroll on this shot at even money odds.

The balls only have to lay in the general area shown.

Use **1 Tip of High Inside English** (Left in this case). Aim to hit the Object Ball 1/4 Full and shoot **HARD**.

The Object Ball must be **spinning** when it hits the 3rd rail to score.

PUTTING THE BITE ON FATS

In Houston, **John "Cannonball Lefty" Chapman**, as expected, was battering Fats nightly. Fats was playing One–Pocket, eight to seven and losing badly. The most unusual part of this particular story came later, when Fats was entertaining pool audiences at tournaments and trade shows around the country — especially when Cannonball happened to be in attendance.

Then Fats told a different story. Fats claimed he had beaten Cannonball in Houston so badly that he had to change his name from Cannonball to "B. B." (The ammo we used to shoot out of the old, Daisy Air Rifles.).

The amazing thing was how Fats could get Chapman to authenticate the lie. Cannonball would agree to whatever tale Fats told about how badly he was trounced by the Fat Man. What people didn't know, was that cooperating with Fats turned the "bite-light" on.

Cannonball would secretly meet Fats later and pick up a nice "bite" (non-payback loan) for his trouble and earlier humiliation.

I can't fault Cannonball for not exposing Fats because I was guilty of the same crime. When I was a kid I got a $20 bite from Fatty in Johnston City.

Whatever else might have been said about him, the Fatman was an easy touch. I never paid the $20 back, but believe me, Fatty got his money's worth.

From then on, whenever Fatty saw me, and he was always surrounded by people — nobody drew a crowd like Fatty, he would launch into outrageous lies about playing in Chicago and beating some champion 50 games in a row, running 100 balls one-handed or going eight and out 22 straight games.

Then the Fatman called on me, saying, "You don't believe me? Well, ask the kid. He's from Chicago. He was there when I did all that. — Am I telling it like it is, kid?"

Naturally, I never had the balls to dispute him and I would always meekly agree with whatever nonsense he was feeding the fold. I have never figured how Fats could get everybody to second his bullshit.

At Johnston City, he even got the great **Luther "Wimpy" Lassiter** to admit that he once shit all over himself because Fatty had beaten him so badly. Fats asserted that "Wimpy's" backer had to take him to the Army-Navy store next door to get him a whole new outfit. He even got "Wimpy" to say he had shit into his shoes.

"Wimpy" probably thought that if he disputed Fatty, Fats would say something worse— what could be worse, I can't imagine— but Wimpy just took his medicine and hoped Fatty would go to work on somebody else.

Now don't get me wrong, I adored Fatty. I hung on his every word like a lovesick puppy. Minnesota Fats (aka New York Fats) was probably the most phenomenal personality I have ever encountered. After being around him, for weeks afterward I tried to talk and act like him.

All things aside, the Fatman played One-Pocket for big money pretty crisply. He ran eight and out faster and more perfectly than maybe anybody. Once he made the first hard shot, the next seven seemed like he was shooting at all hangers. The long hard, off-angle shot, was the only thing that separated him from the really top players.

One other thing of note, Fats was a hellova banker in his day. A young "Bugs" Rucker gave him a ball, eight to seven, and beat him in Johnston City. That wasn't anything to be ashamed of. "Bugs" could give just about anybody a ball.

BUGS GOES BALLISTIC

Spaeth's Pocket

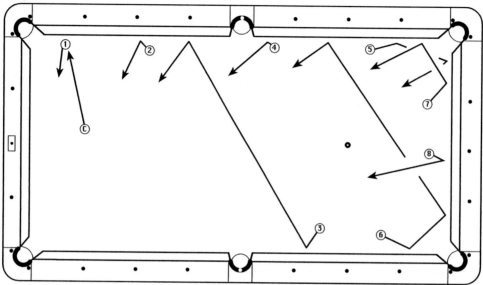

Rucker's Pocket

JOEY SPAETH BECOMES A BELIEVER

When "Bugs" played Fats, Joey "The Cincinnati Kid" Spaeth was staking him. A great player himself, Joey did not often back other players. However, Spaeth just came from Chicago where he had the misfortune to have played Rucker.

Joey instantly became a convert to the Bugs Rucker fan club when, in a game of One–Pocket, with Spaeth only needing one ball to win and everything seemingly out of play, Bugs banked all of the remaining balls into his pocket to win the game. Joey had never seen anything like it before, and I personally have never seen or heard anything like it since.

———————————————●———————————————

The balls are numbered in the order they were banked. 1-ball Cross-corner — follow off the rail for a bank on the 2–ball. Follow for a twice cross–corner on the 3–ball. Stop on the 3–ball and bank the 4-ball cross–corner and stop the Cue Ball again.

Next shoot the 5–ball two rails off the long rail and come out slightly for a 3-rail bank on the 6–ball. Shoot the 7–ball two rails into the corner and bank the 8–ball straight back off the short rail. Then Rucker collected the cheese.

BUGS SCORES A BULLSEYE ON THE RIFLEMAN

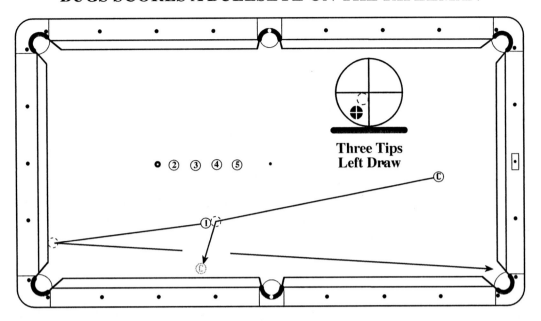

**Three Tips
Left Draw**

In Johnston City, Illinois, Bugs spotted Hall of Famer Buddy Hall two balls — playing banks 10 to 8 — and won the money.

Perhaps you think maybe Buddy played badly — he didn't. Buddy made every makeable ball he shot at, played dead-nuts safeties, never dogged anything and still lost every game.

That was the kind of bank speed the mighty Bugs had.

The bank above is the shot that probably broke Buddy's heart.

When Bugs called the bank, Buddy leaped off the chair to see what-in-hell Bugs was about to do to him. Buddy thought he had left Bugs safe because there is a tough to beat kiss on this shot.

HOW TO MAKE IT

Use extreme (3 Tips) low, Left–Hand English (reverse). Hard Speed.

The Cue Ball ducks inside the returning Object Ball beating the kiss.

The Object Ball shortens off the rail and goes into the pocket.

Bugs then picked off the "fence" to run the game out.

DETROIT WHITEY

In 1961 the venerable **Bensingers Billiard Academy** closed their Loop location on Randolph Street and were in the process of moving to the North Side of Chicago at Clark Street and Diversey Avenue.

While **Bensingers** was revamping, all the action migrated to a bowling alley with about 15 pool tables called **20th Century Lanes** located at Belmont and Cicero Avenues. The place stayed open 24 hours, so there was action aplenty.

The great **Detroit Whitey (Eddie Beauchene)** graced us with his presence for a couple of weeks. Whitey was a top player back then. He had a fat bankroll and Whitey was spotting everybody (giving up a handicap).

I was a "pool nut" then and was totally captivated by Whitey's fearless shooting and flashy showmanship.

There are many stories about Whitey, but he was such a unique character that no story could ever do him justice. You had to see Whitey in action to believe him.

One night a contingent of black players from the South Side came to **20th Century Lanes.** They were led by a then unknown Leonard "Bugs" Rucker. Bugs challenged Whitey to a game of bank pool, and they agreed to play for $40.

Whitey's specialty was 9-ball, but he was a skilled banker nonetheless. Unbeknown to Whitey, it took six of Bugs's backers to come up with the $40. Singles, deuces and fins were gathered in a pile until the $40 was finally put up.

Bugs had only one barrel to play. Needless to say, Rucker won the first game and doubled up to $80 and kept doubling up and kept banking the lights out.

Whitey had never seen anybody bank like Bugs before, except maybe Eddie Taylor.

It was a slaughter, but Whitey wouldn't quit. Whitey was mesmerized and kept paying off until he finally went broke.

When Bugs banked in the final ball, Whitey turned his back to him, pulled his pants down, *including his shorts*, pulled his cheeks apart and said, "Go ahead and fuck me, you black son–of–a–bitch, you've been fucking me all night anyway."

Hilarious as it was to the sweaters, there were women in the bowling alley and some of them caught Whitey's outrageous act and raised a big stink about it.

The owners soon chased all the hustlers out of the joint, never to return, and the place began closing early.

Big money action never happened at **20th Century Lanes** again, but **Bensingers** reopened a month or two later and I set up shop there for the next 20 years. Bugs went on to become a world bank champion.

AUTOMATIC CROSS CORNER

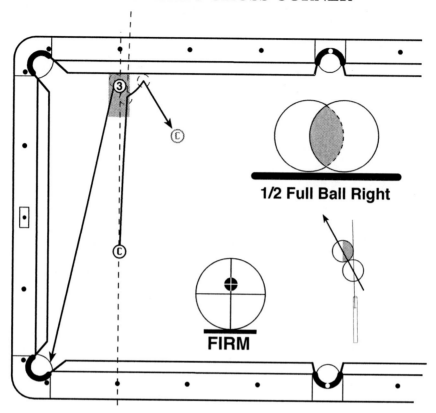

1/2 Full Ball Right

FIRM

This is an easy bank to remember. Both the Cue Ball and the Object Ball are on a line between the first diamonds on the long rail, and the Object Ball is in the grey area within a diamond space of the long rail.

The actual diamond count for a natural bank would call for a 3/4 full hit. However, because of **Collision-Induced–English** and **Throw,** a 3/4 ball hit lands the Object Ball somewhat short of the pocket.

To make this shot, we must subtract 1/4 ball from the Aim to allow for the effects of *Acquired English*.

This means a 1/2 ball hit is required to score.

AUTOMATIC STRAIGHT BACK

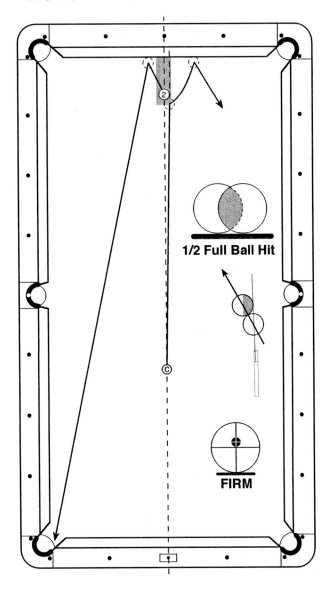

1/2 Full Ball Hit

FIRM

Here's another version of the half-ball aim used for the cross-corner shot on the preceding page.

Since the distance to the pocket is doubled, the half-ball hit scores from two diamonds away on a long bank.

AUTOMATIC CROSS CORNER

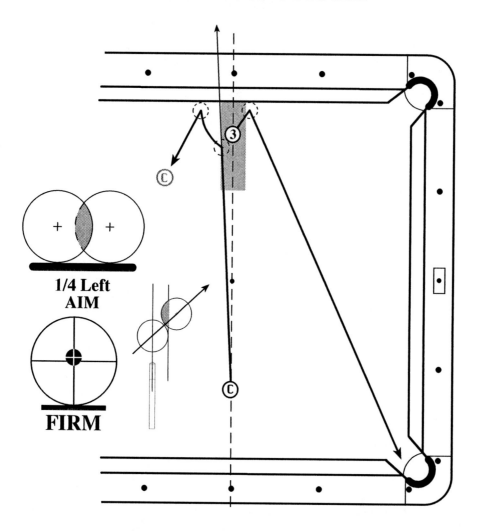

1/4 Left AIM

FIRM

This time the natural bank angle would require a 1/2 ball hit.

However, **Collision-Induced-Throw** requires an adjustment to score. Using a 1/4 ball hit overcomes the *Acquired English* and sends the ball home.

These reference banks will tune your bank sense for similar shots.

As long as the Object Ball is in the grey area and the Cue Ball is on the dashed line, this bank can be made using a 1/4 ball hit with **FIRM Speed**.

AUTOMATIC CROSS CORNER

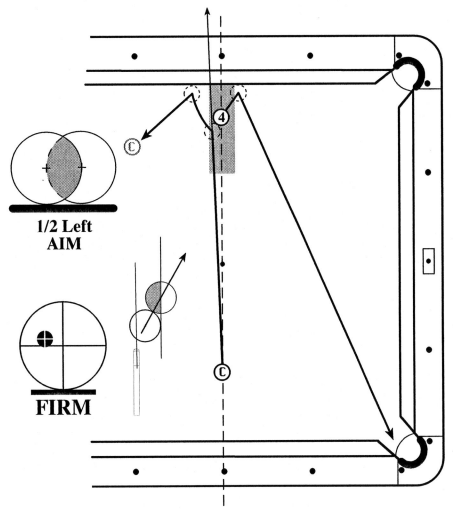

1/2 Left AIM

FIRM

Here's another way to make this Automatic Cross-Corner.

Instead of adjusting the Aim for **Collision–Induced–Throw**, use a 1/2 Ball Hit and 2 Tips of Left-English to *throw* the Object Ball into the pocket.

Use **FIRM SPEED**.

AUTOMATIC CROSS CORNER

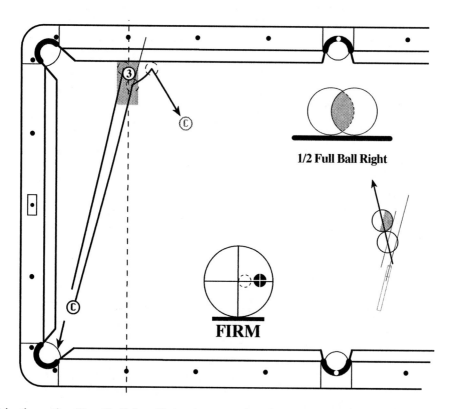

1/2 Full Ball Right

FIRM

This time the Cue Ball is off the Automatic Line by a full Diamond. The bank can be made with a **1/2 Ball Hit Using 2 Tips of Outside English** (Right-English in this case) and **Firm Speed**.

Cross–side banks work exactly the same way.

AUTOMATIC CROSS CORNER

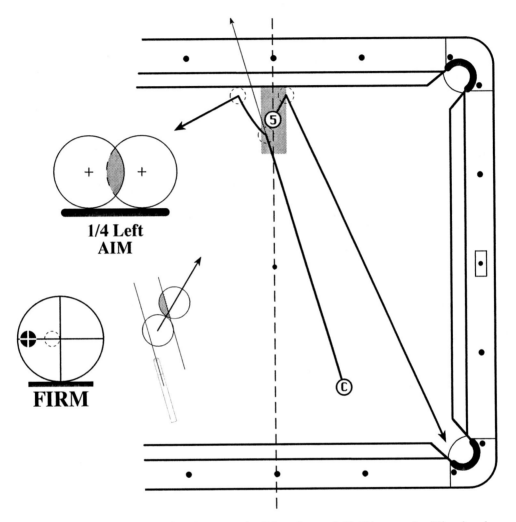

**1/4 Left
AIM**

FIRM

Here the Cue Ball is off the Automatic Line by a full Diamond. The bank can be made by using **3 Tips of Outside English** (Left-English this time) with **Firm Speed**.

The **Outside English** cancels the **Collision-Induced-English** and **Throw** and sends the ball into the pocket.

AUTOMATIC CROSS CORNER

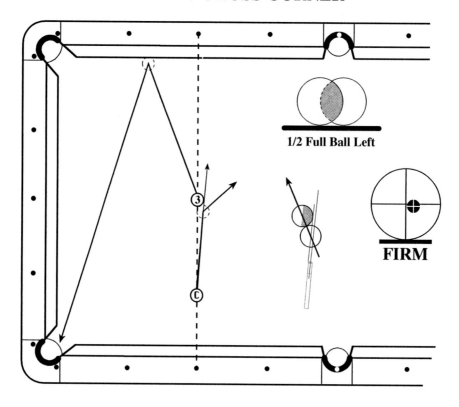

1/2 Full Ball Left

FIRM

When there is a straight line-up for a spotted ball, use a **1/2 Ball Hit** with **1 Tip of Outside English** to eliminate **Collision-Induced-Throw** and send the ball home.

ENGLISH AND DISTANCE

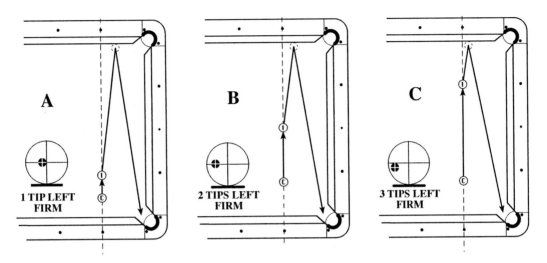

A

1 TIP LEFT
FIRM

B

2 TIPS LEFT
FIRM

C

3 TIPS LEFT
FIRM

The farther from the cushion the Object Ball lies, the greater the angle english will create.

A — From 3 Diamonds away **1 Tip of English** is enough to send the bank cross-corner.

B — From 2 Diamonds away it takes **2 Tips of English** to do the job.

C — From 1 Diamond away **3 Tips of English** is needed to send the bank cross-corner.

The farther an Object Ball travels to a cushion the more the english can **Throw** the ball into the correct angle. From closer there is less space for **Throw** and more english must take effect **on** the cushion to create the correct bank angle.

AUTOMATIC STRAIGHT BACK

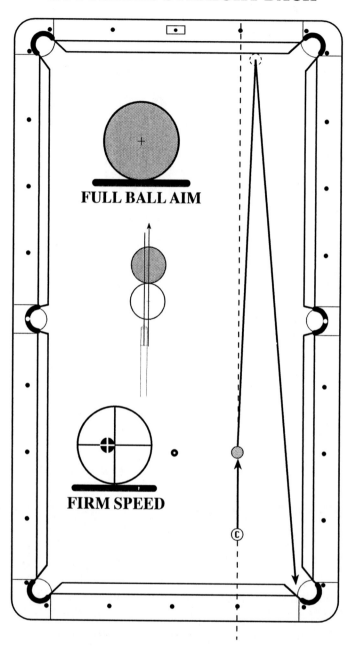

FULL BALL AIM

FIRM SPEED

Use **FIRM SPEED**.

When the balls are lined up 1 Diamond away from the corner, hitting dead Full with **1 Tip Outside English** makes the bank.

AUTOMATIC STRAIGHT BACK

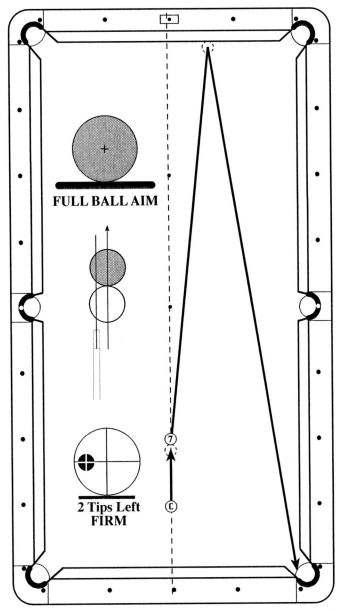

FULL BALL AIM

**2 Tips Left
FIRM**

When you have a dead straight shot at a spotted ball, hit the Object Ball full in the face with **2 Tips Outside English** (Left in this case). The side-spin throws and applies a small amount of favorable rotation to the Object Ball that sends it into the corner.

On some equipment, you must cut the Object Ball a hair toward the pocket to score.

AUTOMATIC CROSS CORNER

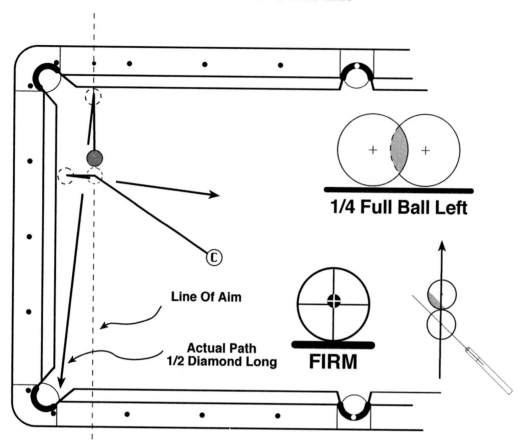

1/4 Full Ball Left

Line Of Aim

Actual Path
1/2 Diamond Long   **FIRM**

Those who were paying attention will notice that this **Automatic Passover Bank** was demonstrated in the section proving **Acquired English** (p. 32-35).

A **1/4 Full Hit** played *square* into the cushion applies enough **Acquired English** to **Throw** the Object Ball 1/2 Diamond Long of the geometric Aim.

AUTOMATIC 3 Rail In The Side

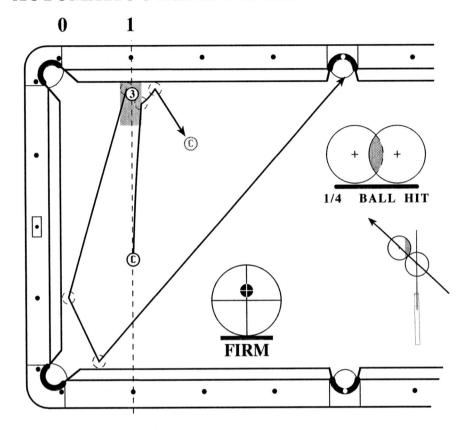

Here's another nice little trick you can do with an **AUTOMATIC CROSS-CORNER** position.

Instead of playing a 1/2 Ball Hit for a Cross-Corner shot, **SUBTRACT** 1/4 ball from the aim and play the bank 3 rails in the side.

Using a 1/4 Full Hit with **FIRM SPEED** and No English drives the ball 3 rails into the side.

BANKING WITH THE BEARD

ONE IN THE SIDE

A — C
EASY SPEED

D
EASY SPEED
1 TIP OUTSIDE ENGLISH

Sight these shots **THRU** the Long Rail Diamonds to **OPPOSITE** the designated End Rail Diamonds.

Bank A: Sight **THRU** Diamond 1.0 on the Long Rail to **OPPOSITE** End Rail Diamond 3.5. Use Easy Speed.

Bank B: Sight **THRU** Diamond 2.0 on the Long Rail to **OPPOSITE** End Rail Diamond 3.0. Use Easy Speed.

Bank C: Sight **THRU** Diamond 3.0 on the Long Rail to **OPPOSITE** End Rail Diamond 2.5. Use Easy Speed.

Bank D: Sight **THRU** Diamond 4.0 on the Long Rail to **OPPOSITE** End Rail Diamond 2.0. Use Easy Speed with 1 Tip of Outside English (Left–Hand English in this example).

Use the standard adjustments when you must Cut or Passover one of these banks.

If the alignment is good and you are careful, these banks are no worse than a 50/50 shot.

When leaving a tough spot where you just won the money and you sense there will be trouble from the losers, send whoever **did not** do the playing out first. They won't follow him as long as you are still in the joint with the money.

Your associate's instructions are simple: Get the car, pull it right in front of the place with the motor running, the passenger door open, and the car pointed towards home.

I once had a partner who left the last part out. He did everything perfect except pull the car out of the parking space. I went outside, jumped in the car, and while he was maneuvering out of the parking space, the bad guys descended, pulled their guns and got in the car. I eventually escaped, with all the cheese, and my life and limb, but that's another story.

The reasoning behind my instructions is sound because tush-hogs will seldom attack inside the joint. They prefer to wait and do their mischief outside where nobody can see anything to call the police about.

Kilroy's Rules Of The Road

2–RAILER UP AND BACK

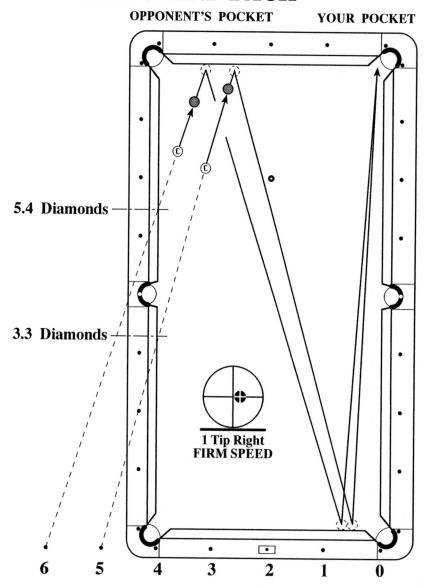

OPPONENT'S POCKET   **YOUR POCKET**

5.4 Diamonds

3.3 Diamonds

1 Tip Right
FIRM SPEED

6   5   4   3   2   1   0

Up-and-Back 2-Railers work the same way as their cross-table cousins. Shooting on the Natural 2-to-1 Bank Angle with **FIRM SPEED** and 1 Tip of Inside English sends the Object Ball on a 2–Rail trip into your pocket.

2 Rail Cross–Corner

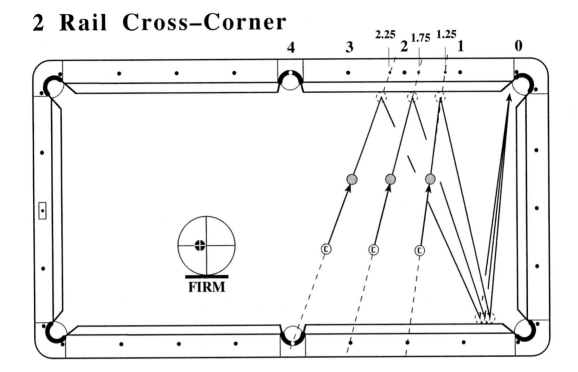

All of these side–to–side two rail shots work the same way.

SPEED: Firm

Use **1 Tip of Outside–English** to insure the correct action off the second rail.

These shots work with Natural Banks, Cut Banks and Passover Banks.

The closer the Object Ball is to the first rail the easier it is for the ball to break long on the second rail, rather than reversing and running short.

The Landing Point on the second rail is within two ball spaces for all three shots.

SMALL ADJUSTMENTS

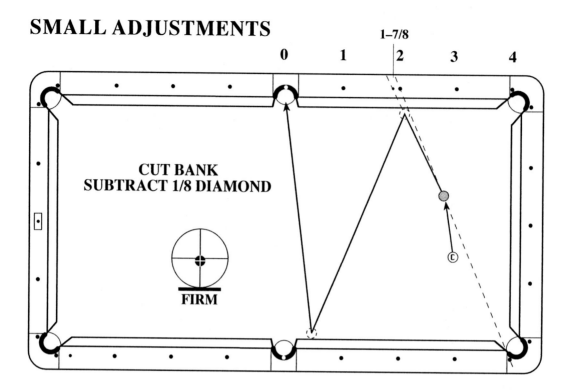

For deadly accuracy Subtracting 1/8 Diamond from Cut Banks puts these shots on a bulls eye path for 2–railers in the Sides and Corners.

SMALL ADJUSTMENTS

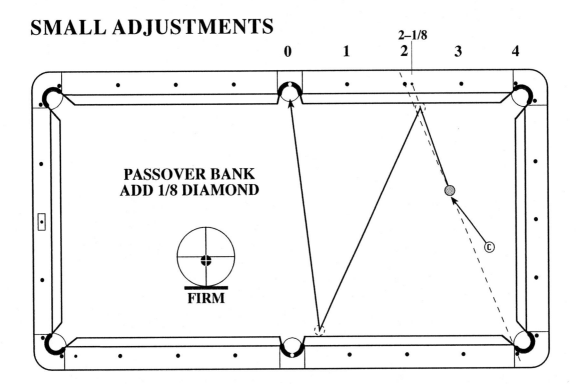

For deadly accuracy adding 1/8 Diamond to Passover Banks 1/8 Diamond puts these banks on a dead center path into the pocket.

On a 4–1/2 x 9 foot table 1/8 Diamond equals about .70 ball space (1.56").

Making this small compensation for **Collision-Induced-Throw** puts the Object Ball on track for a 2–rail shot.

SMALL ADJUSTMENTS

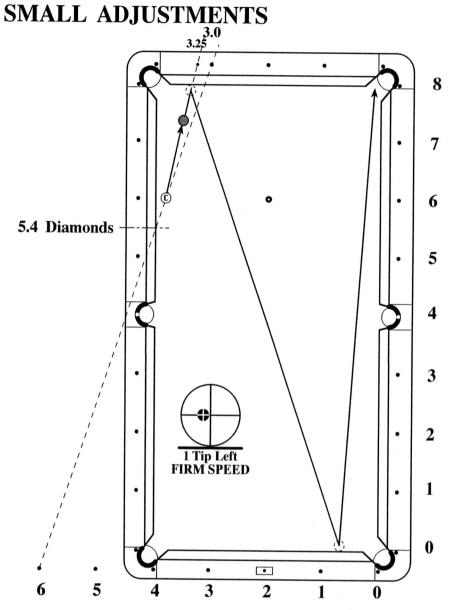

When a bank lies on a path straight-into the first cushion and .25 Diamonds short of the Natural Angle, hitting the Object Ball dead in the face using 1 Tip of Outside English (left in this example) sends the Object Ball on a two-rail bank track.

SMALL ADJUSTMENTS

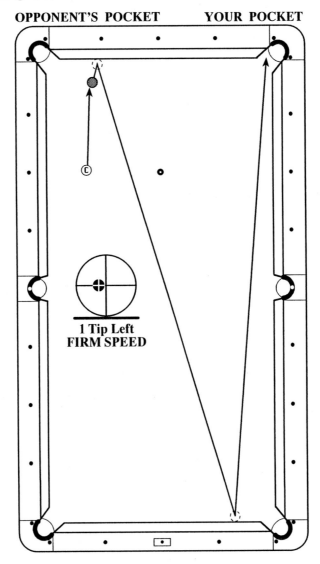

When you have to cut the Object Ball into the Natural Angle you must use 1 Tip of Outside English to compensate for *Acquired English* which would send the shot far short of the desired path.

Using **FIRM SPEED** and 1 Tip of Outside English sends the Object Ball on a two-rail track to your pocket.

2 In Side Short Rail First

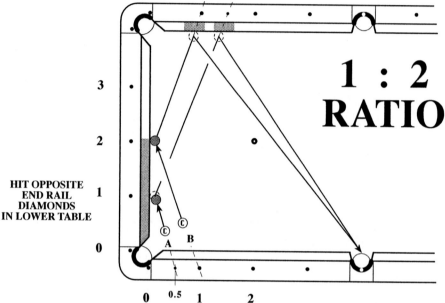

These banks are figured on a **1 : 2 Ratio**. This is to say, the Long Rail Diamond numbers are **MULTIPLIED** by 2 to find the Short Rail Targets. For instance, the Bank Track from Long Rail Diamond position 1 sights **OPPOSITE** End Rail Diamond 2.0 (1.0 x 2 = 2.0).

Long Rail numbers are sighted **THRU** the Diamond positions while the Short Rail Targets are **OPPOSITE** the Diamond positions up to Diamond 2.0. After Diamond 2.0 shots are sighted **THRU** the end rail Diamonds.

    A: Bank on a line running **Thru Diamond .5** on the long rail to an imaginary ball **Opposite** End Rail **Diamond 1**.

Bank the Object Ball **Thru Diamond 1.5** on 2nd rail.

    B: Bank on a line running **Thru Diamond 1** on the long rail to an imaginary ball **Opposite** End Rail **Diamond 2**.

Bank the Object Ball **Thru Diamond 1** on 2nd rail.

                           Use **EASY speed** on all shots.

2 In Side Short Rail First

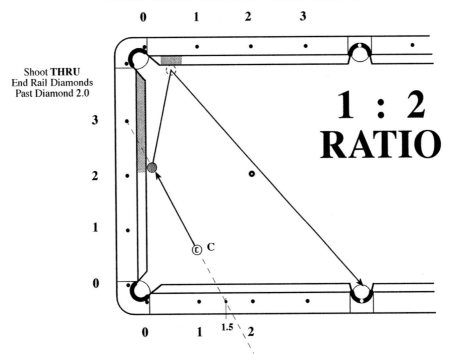

C: Past **Diamond 2.0** Sight **THRU** the Short Rail Diamonds.

Bank this shot on a line running **Thru Diamond 1.5** on the long rail **Thru** Short Rail **Diamond 3**.

It is especially helpful to pay attention to the bank path into the second-rail on successful shots. The second cushion contact and the Ball Action on the Object Ball determine the outcome of these shots.

Use **EASY SPEED** on all shots.

2 RAILER IN SIDE — Long Rail First

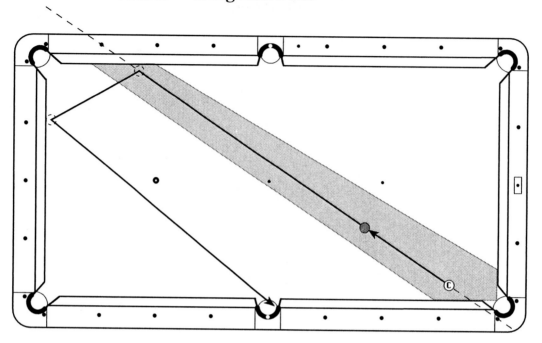

These 2–Railers in the side work best in the grey area.

Use **FIRM Speed** and **Sight Thru** Diamond 1.0 on the long rail.

TWO RAILER OFF THE SPOT

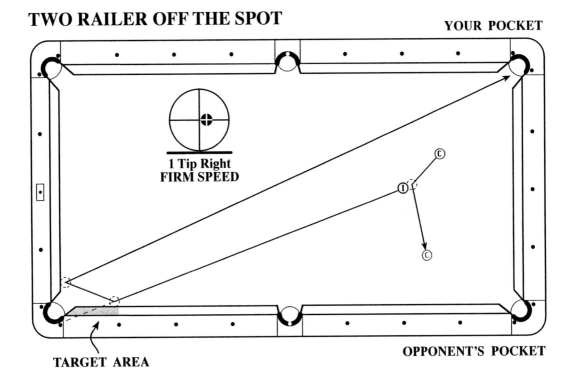

YOUR POCKET

1 Tip Right
FIRM SPEED

TARGET AREA

OPPONENT'S POCKET

When an Object Ball is on the Foot Spot you can make a 2-Rail shot to your corner by driving the ball **THRU** the grey Target Area. Any hit from the Foot Spot **THRU** the grey area will work.

1 Tip Inside English with **Firm Speed** must be used to adjust the bank angle off the second cushion.

A 1/2 to 3/4 Full Cut Angle works best.

A Straight On Full Ball Hit works with a Tip of Inside English to tighten up the bank path.

A Passover shot won't work because the ball action applies the wrong english to the Object Ball.

When I first saw great players like **"Champagne Eddie" Kelly** make this shot I thought they used their extraordinary stroking skill to send the ball home. Since then I've discovered that the natural action of a Cut Bank angle makes this a relatively simple shot.

3 Rails In Side End Rail First

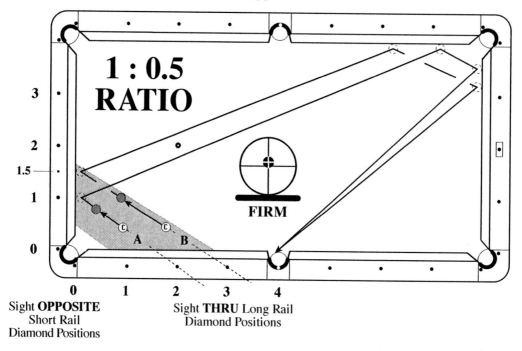

BANK A — 2 x 0.5 = 1.0 = **Side Pocket**

BANK B — 3 x 0.5 = 1.5 = **Side Pocket**

1 : 0.5 RATIO

Three railers in the side off the end rail are impressive, but on many tables this shot is no worse than a 50/50 shot in the grey area.

The range between Diamond 1 and Diamond 3 (grey area) is where this shot is best.

Use **FIRM** Speed.

EXTENDED 3 RAILER

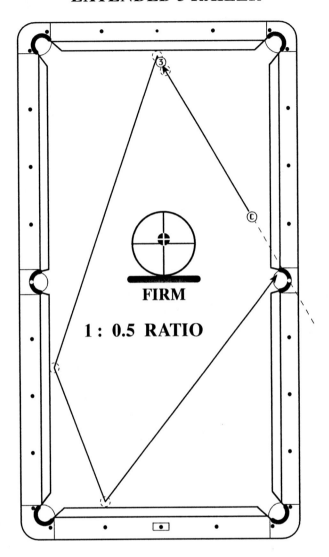

FIRM

1 : 0.5 RATIO

3 RAILS IN THE SIDE SYSTEM

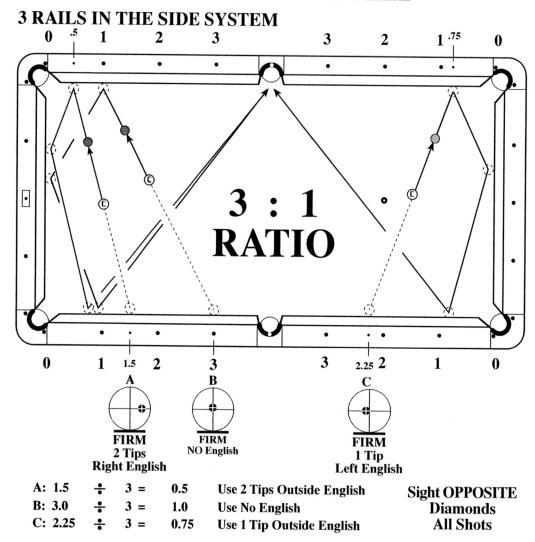

A: 1.5 ÷ 3 = 0.5   Use 2 Tips Outside English   **Sight OPPOSITE**
B: 3.0 ÷ 3 = 1.0   Use No English   **Diamonds**
C: 2.25 ÷ 3 = 0.75 Use 1 Tip Outside English   **All Shots**

3 : 1 RATIO

Three in the side shots are calculated on a **3 : 1 Ratio**. In other words the Target Diamond on the first bank cushion is 1/3 of the starting Diamond.

Shots are sighted between the centers of **Ghost Balls** exactly opposite the relative Diamond positions. For example, **Bank A** runs from **OPPOSITE** Diamond position 1.5 to **OPPOSITE** Diamond position 0.5 on the first bank cushion for a **3 : 1 Ratio**.

The Ratio for these banks is always **3 : 1**.

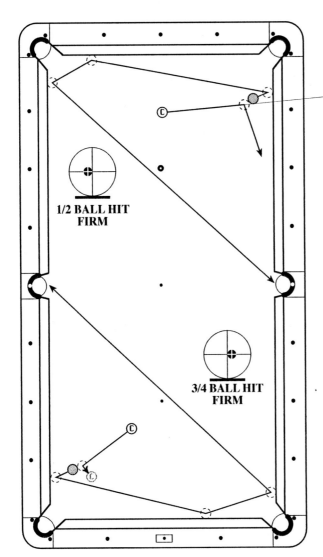

3 RAILS IN SIDE

1/2 Ball Cut Bank

Problem: Object Ball Tends To Run Short

Solution: Use 1 Tip Reverse English. **Firm Speed**.

The Object Ball breaks longer off the 3rd rail

3 RAILS IN SIDE

3/4 Ball Partial Passover Bank

Problem: Object Ball Tends To Run Short

Solution: Use 1 Tip Outside English. **Firm Speed.**

The Object Ball breaks longer off the 3rd rail.

3 In Side Short Rail First

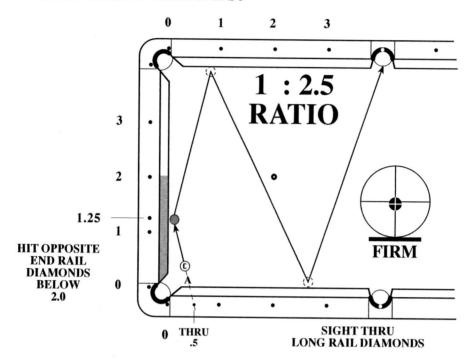

These 3 railers require a **1 : 2.5 Ratio**.

Bank A: Sight this bank on a line running **Thru Diamond .5** on the Long Rail to an imaginary ball **Opposite** End Rail **Diamond 1.25**. (0.5 x 2.5 = 1.25)

3 In Side Short Rail First

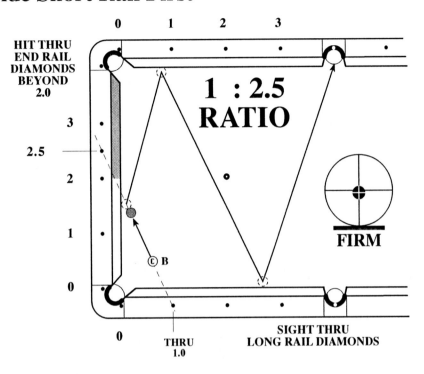

Bank B: **ABOVE** Diamond 2.0 (grey area) on the End Rail we sight **THRU** the designated Diamonds.

Bank on a line running **Thru Diamond 1** on the Long Rail Thru End Rail **Diamond 2.5**. (1.0 x 2.5 = 2.5)

Use **FIRM Speed** on all shots.

4 RAILS IN SIDE LONG RAIL FIRST

In Lower Half of Table Sight **OPPOSITE** Indicated Diamonds

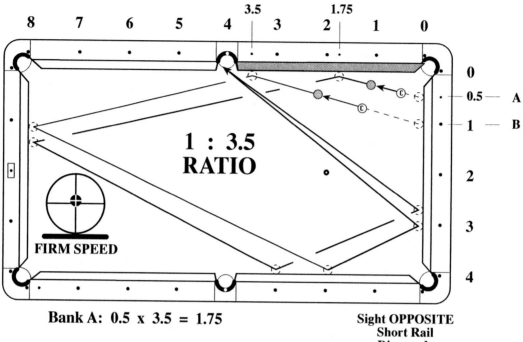

Bank A: 0.5 x 3.5 = 1.75

Bank B: 1.0 x 3.5 = 3.50

Sight OPPOSITE
Short Rail
Diamonds

Drilling 4–Railers in the sides was a specialty of **Truman Hogue**. When one of these shots came up Hogue only took a couple of seconds to line up and send the Object Ball flying around the table into the back of the side pocket with a resounding **thwack!**

Use a **1 : 3.5 Ratio** and remember to sight shots **OPPOSITE** the Long Rail Diamonds in the lower half of the table.

Use **FIRM SPEED** with no english.

4 RAILS IN SIDE LONG RAIL FIRST

In Upper Half of Table Sight **THRU** Indicated Diamonds

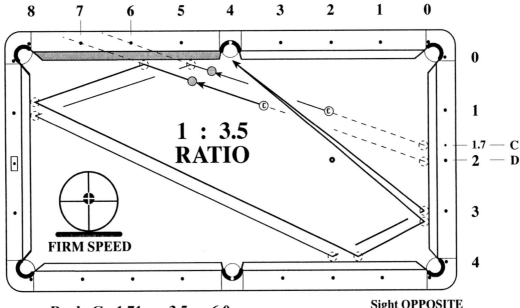

1 : 3.5 RATIO

FIRM SPEED

Bank C: 1.71 x 3.5 = 6.0

Bank D: 2.0   x 3.5 = 7.0

**Sight OPPOSITE
Short Rail Diamonds
All Shots**

Sight shots **THRU** the Long Rail Diamonds in the upper half of the table (grey area).

Use **FIRM SPEED** with no english.

4 RAILS IN SIDE— THE HARD WAY

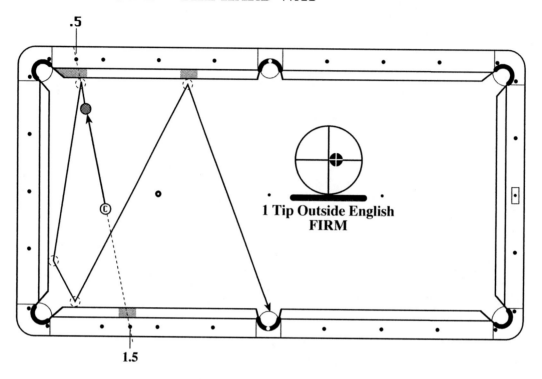

1 Tip Outside English
FIRM

This shot only works in the limited area shown. There is very little leeway for adjustments.

Use **1 Tip Outside English** with **FIRM SPEED**.

SYSTEMOLOGY

There are a number of reasons why a table may not bank according to the systems in this book. First, the rubber on some tables produces different rebound angles than the norm. If the rubber deteriorates with age, the bank angles also change. Sometimes you might have to cope with high humidity, which alters the way a cushion plays.

When a system does not work here are a few adjustments to try.

Begin by using the tools provided in the solutions for Natural, Cut and Passover Banks (p 38-56) and using the Plus & Minus Charts (p 92-98) to solve the equations.

Adjust the aim by **1/4 Ball Hits**, use **1/4 Diamond Increments** and **1 Tip Changes In English** to accommodate the errant cushion. For example, if banks are landing 1/4 Diamond Short, try subtracting 1/4 Diamond from the cushion target. You can also add 1 Tip of outside English to overcome the shortened bank angle. Changing the speed according to the **Easy**, **Firm** and **Hard Speed** measurements may also help.

Experimenting with these methods may enable you to harmonize your aiming and execution with the reality of the defective rubber.

Another reason systems fail is because the player has a poor mental image of the shot. Instead of shooting the bank according to the formula, which is correct, the shooter unconsciously adjusts the angle according to flawed mental imagery and almost always misses.

I had this problem myself on certain shots. When the bank came up, the right way to play it looked totally wrong, but when I followed my instinct I usually missed. I had to **force** myself to play the bank properly until my mental image conformed to the reality of the table.

If a system does not look right, **force** yourself to execute according to the instructions. You will usually be pleasantly surprised to see the ball disappear into the pocket. If you continue shooting a shot correctly, before long your mental imagery will conform to the true bank angles.

Having an accurate mental picture of a bank is a great help in making the shot. Good mental imagery improves aiming and execution.

2 RAILS IN CORNER, SHORT RAIL FIRST

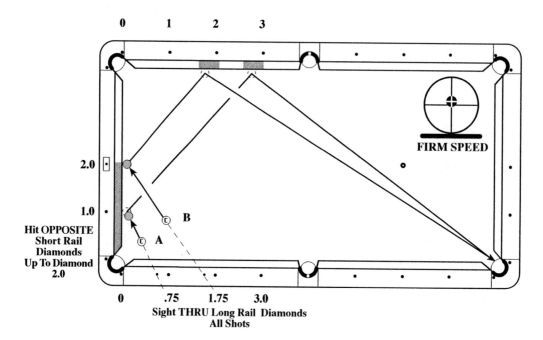

Sight **THRU** the indicated Long Rail Diamonds to a point **OPPOSITE** the designated Diamond count on the End Rail up to Diamond 2.0 (grey area).

Bank balls into the grey target areas on the second cushion for consistency.

> **Bank A: Sight THRU Long Rail 0.75 to OPPOSITE 1.0 on the Short Rail.**

> **Bank B: Sight THRU Long Rail 1.75 to OPPOSITE 2.0 on the Short Rail.**

2 RAILS IN CORNER, SHORT RAIL FIRST

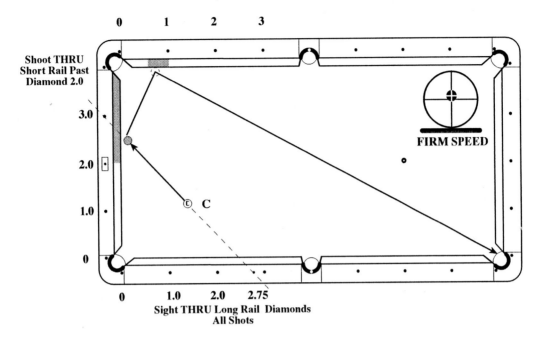

Past Diamond 2.0 on the end rail (grey area) sight **THRU** Short Rail Diamonds.

Bank C: Sight THRU Long Rail 2.75 to THRU 3.0 on the Short Rail.

Use **FIRM SPEED.**

LONG RAIL REFERENCE POINT

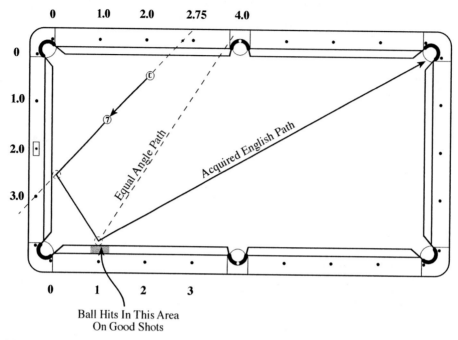

Ball Hits In This Area
On Good Shots

Watching where the Object Ball hits the second cushion on successful shots provides a winning bank path on these shots.

Many good bankers use second-rail aiming points as guides for 2 Rail and 4 Rail Banks. Experience has taught them that hitting certain places on the second rail puts the shot on a bullseye path. After a few attempts, their success rate soars.

Successful banks have a certain sound, shape and ball action. Pay attention to the *spin* the Object Ball has when it hits the second-rail. The ***Acquired-English*** from the first-rail contact widens the angle off the second-rail on these shots more than three Diamond spaces. Without the spin, the bank will not score.

Watch carefully and you can see the Object Ball curve into a scoring path off the second-rail because of the ***Acquired-English***.

Getting a *feel* for the speed, spin and angle required for banks is essential for high–speed play.

When you play a bank, visualize the shot going as you desire. Forming a good mental image of a shot is a great help in increasing your bank percentage.

2 RAILS IN CORNER, SHORT RAIL FIRST

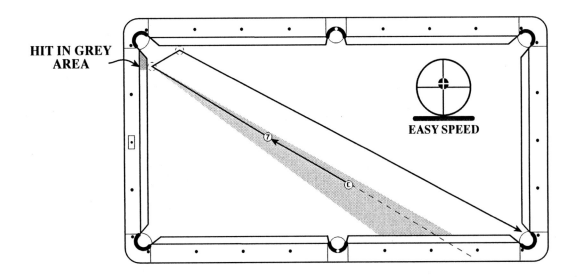

HIT IN GREY AREA

EASY SPEED

Here's a shot you've probably made accidentally more than a few times. When the balls are lined up well, hit the end rail a ball space or so away from the pocket with **EASY SPEED**.

On many tables a near miss into the grey area is a dead shot into the diagonal corner.

2 RAILS IN CORNER

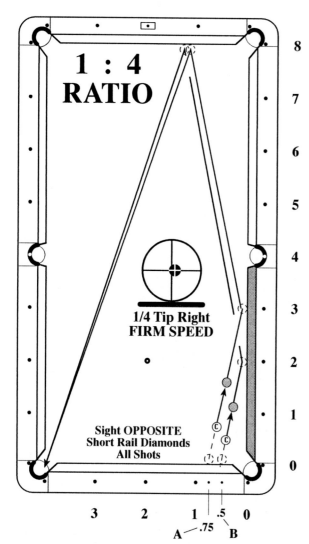

1 : 4 RATIO

Sight OPPOSITE Short Rail Diamonds All Shots

1/4 Tip Right FIRM SPEED

1 : 4 RATIO

The ratio for these shots is 1:4. This is to say, a starting point of 0.5 Diamonds calls for a 2.0 hit on the first-rail. (0.5 x 4 = 2)

The short rail Diamond count for these shots is **OPPOSITE** the relevant Diamond positions.

For example, a bank that originates at .75 Diamonds on the Short Rail requires a hit exactly **OPPOSITE** Diamond 3.0 on the first cushion. (4 x 0.75 = 3.0)

There is always a 1:4 Ratio between the Short rail count and the Long Rail contact point.

In the Lower Half of the table sight OPPOSITE indicated Diamonds.

BANK A: The calculation for a bank from **OPPOSITE** End Rail Diamond 0.75 is sighted to **OPPOSITE** Diamond 3.0 on the first cushion. (.75 x 4 = 3.0)

BANK B: Likewise, a bank from **OPPOSITE** Short Rail Diamond 0.5 is sighted to **OPPOSITE** Diamond 2.0 (0.5 x 4 = 2.0) on the long rail.

1/4 Tip of opposite english is used to insure the correct ball action off the second rail.

2 RAILS IN CORNER

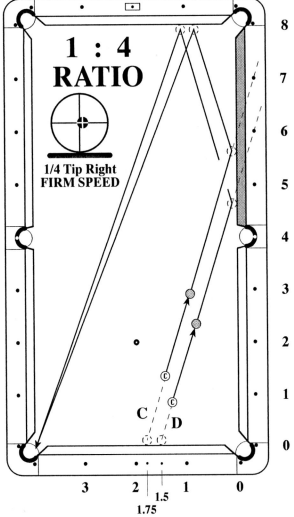

1 : 4 RATIO

In Upper Half of Table Sight THRU Indicated Diamonds.

When the Indicated Diamond count is in the upper half of the table (i.e. Diamond 5 — 7) the bank must be sighted **THRU** the appropriate Diamond.

The same **1:4 Ratio** is used to figure banks in the upper table, but shots are sighted **THRU** the 1st rail Diamonds.

Short Rail starting points are always **OPPOSITE** the Diamonds.

Use **FIRM SPEED** with 1/4 Tip of Opposite English (Right-English in these examples.).

BANK C — 1.75 x 4 = 7

BANK D — 1.5 x 4 = 6

Use **FIRM SPEED** and 1/4 Tip Opposite English (Right-English in this case) to get the proper action off the second cushion.

3 Rails In Corner End Rail First

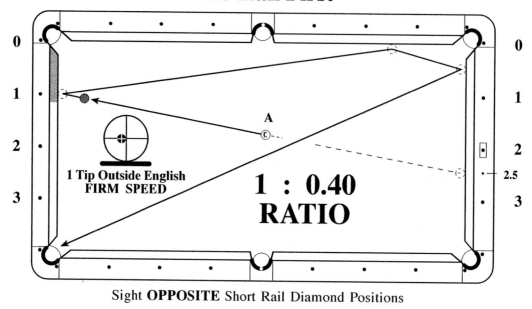

1 Tip Outside English
FIRM SPEED

1 : 0.40
RATIO

Sight **OPPOSITE** Short Rail Diamond Positions

BANK A — 2.5 x 0.40   =   1.0 =   Corner Pocket

1 : 0.40 RATIO

Three railers in the **CORNER** off the end rail are persuasive.

Use a **1 : 0.40 Ratio** figured **OPPOSITE** the end rail Diamonds.

First-rail targets between 0.5 and 1.0 Diamonds offer the best chance on these stunning banks.

Use **1 Tip Outside English** with **FIRM SPEED**.

3 Rails In Corner End Rail First

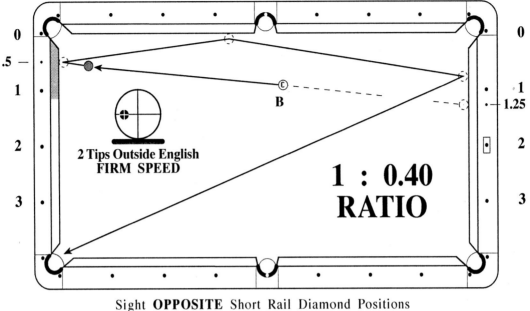

Sight **OPPOSITE** Short Rail Diamond Positions

BANK B — 1.25 x 0.40   =   0.5   =   CornerPocket

Shooting into the grey area provides the best opportunity to make these majestic banks.

Use **2 Tips Outside English** with **FIRM SPEED**.

UP & BACK: 3 RAILER

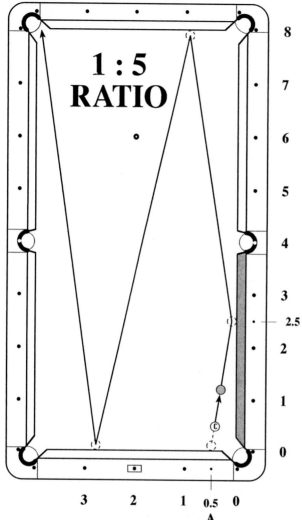

1:5 RATIO

Use a 1:5 Ratio

In the **Lower Table** and Sight **OPPOSITE** the indicated Diamond positions.

Use **HARD Speed** for these shots.

A **1:5 Ratio** puts these shots in the right neck of the woods for scoring.

**In LOWER Half of Table
Sight OPPOSITE
Long Rail Diamond Position**

HARD SPEED

**Always Sight Opposite
End Rail Diamonds**

1 to 5 Ratio

BANK A — 0.5 x 5 = 2.5

UP & BACK: 3 RAILER

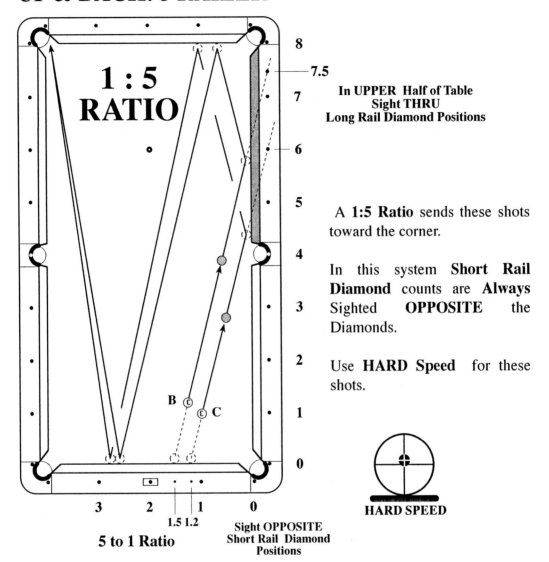

1 : 5 RATIO

8
— 7.5
7
6
5
4
3
2
1
0

In UPPER Half of Table
Sight THRU
Long Rail Diamond Positions

A **1:5 Ratio** sends these shots toward the corner.

In this system **Short Rail Diamond** counts are **Always** Sighted **OPPOSITE** the Diamonds.

Use **HARD Speed** for these shots.

HARD SPEED

B   C

3   2   1   0

1.5 1.2

5 to 1 Ratio

Sight OPPOSITE
Short Rail Diamond
Positions

BANK B — 1.5 x 5 = 7.5

BANK C — 1.2 x 5 = 6.0

4 BAGGERS

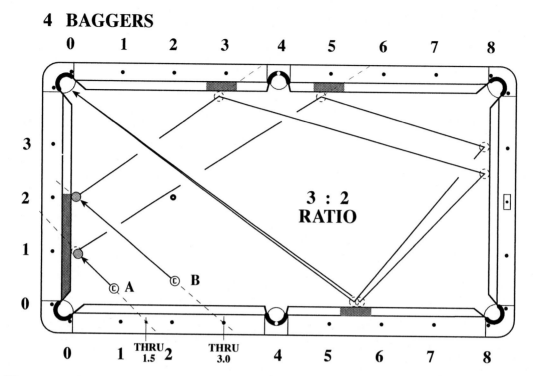

The approach angle to the first-rail for these 4–rail shots has a **3:2 RATIO**.

Up to Diamond 2.0 sight shots **OPPOSITE** the end rail Diamonds.

**HARD
NO English**

Bank A: Sight from **THRU** 1.5 to **OPPOSITE** 1.0.

Bank the Object Ball on a line **THRU** the grey area near Diamond 5.0 on the long rail.

Bank B: Sight from **THRU** 3.0 to **OPPOSITE** 2.0 on the Short Rail.

Bank the Object Ball on a line **THRU** the grey area near Diamond 3.5 on the Long Rail.

The key to making these shots is visualizing yourself driving the Object Ball **THRU** the grey areas on the second-rail. The angle into the second cushion is critical for scoring. Once you find the correct path to the second-rail your percentage will go way up.

4 BAGGERS

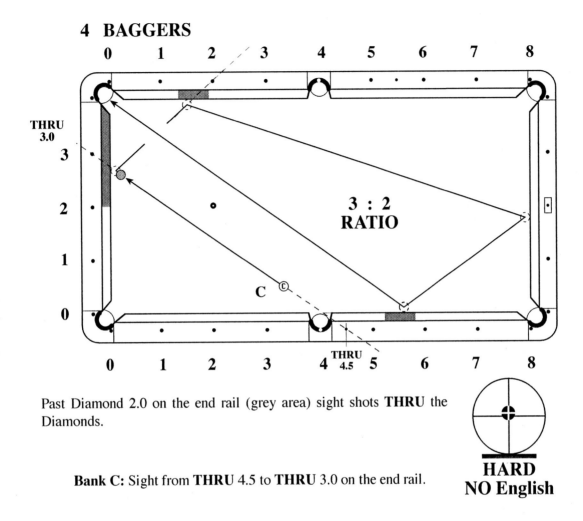

Past Diamond 2.0 on the end rail (grey area) sight shots **THRU** the Diamonds.

Bank C: Sight from **THRU** 4.5 to **THRU** 3.0 on the end rail.

HARD
NO English

Bank the Object Ball on a line into the grey area near Diamond 2 on the Long Rail.

5 Rails In Corner

**In Upper Half of Table Sight THRU
Long Rail Diamond Positions**

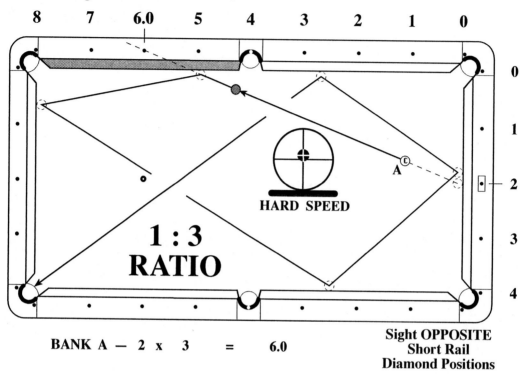

| 8 | 7 | 6.0 | 5 | 4 | 3 | 2 | 1 | 0 |

HARD SPEED

**1 : 3
RATIO**

A©

BANK A — 2 x 3   =   6.0

**Sight OPPOSITE
Short Rail
Diamond Positions**

If you sight the shot carefully there's a good chance of making this spectacular 5–Rail shot.

Shoot **THRU** the indicated Long Rail Diamonds in the Upper Table. (grey area)

5 Rails In Corner

**In Lower Half of Table Sight OPPOSITE
Long Rail Diamond Positions**

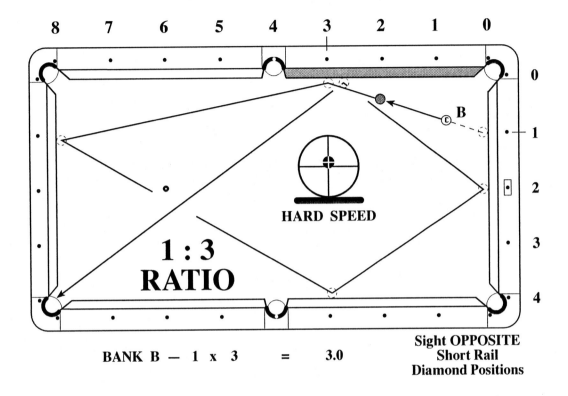

HARD SPEED

**1 : 3
RATIO**

BANK B — 1 x 3   =   3.0

**Sight OPPOSITE
Short Rail
Diamond Positions**

Shoot **OPPOSITE** the Long Rail Diamonds in the Lower Table.

These adjustments are necessary to account for the English the Object Ball Acquires from the cushions.

It takes a hard stroke to drive a ball 5 rails, so don't spare the horsepower.

THEY MIGHT BE GIANTS

Marshall "Tuscaloosa Squirrel" Carpenter was a prime time One–Pocket player in his heyday. Squirrel had the charisma of a movie star and dressed the part wearing impeccable clothing.

When Squirrel walked into a poolroom everyone sat up and took notice, not only because of his fancy dress, but because he was one of the best one–pocket players on the planet and he liked to bet with both hands. It was an all around winning combination for a premier shooter.

At the Jansco Brothers tournament in Johnston City, IL one year, Squirrel had a legendary encounter with a shrewd proposition artist named Brier Spivey.

Spivey came to Jansco's All-Around Hustler Tournament with an unbeatable One-Pocket proposition game. To make things tough on the hustlers Spivey insisted that they play One-Pocket using a 21-ball rack.

These were Spivey's rules:

1. Players had a free break and then played for the pocket they had picked. Any balls made in the player's pocket count.

2. Scoring was on the "rotation" value of the balls (i.e. the 1–ball counted 1 point and the 21–ball counted 21 points).

3. Players were handicapped and played for various scores according to Spivey's estimation of their game. Run of the mill (for Johnston City) players had to shoot for a "rotation" score of around 165 points.

4. Once the handicap was set the player drew three numbers from a pill bottle and the sum of the pills drawn was subtracted from the winning score number. To wit: a player with a 165 handicap might draw a total of, say 15 points, making the goal 150 points.

5. Successful attempts were paid 10-1 on the bet.

Many tried Spivey's game but there were no winners. The conglomeration created by 21 balls made runs almost impossible. None of the hustlers could beat Spivey's proposition.

None, that is, until Squirrel entered the fray. When Squirrel saw the set-up, he innocently asked, "Can I play?"

"Sure,"   Spivey replied, "you have to shoot for 190." (There are 231 points in play.) Ignoring the long odds Spivey set for him, Squirrel threw a C-note on the table and said, "Rack 'em up."

Squirrel proceeded to put on the One-Pocket exhibition of a lifetime by running all 21 balls into his pocket. Squirrel made incredible three–ball bank combinations, bank kiss shots and absolutely astounding moves to overcome the congestion created by 21 balls. It was a tour de force.

After his spectacular runout, Squirrel nonchalantly asked, "Want to go again, I'll let the whole thousand ride."

"No, you won't!" Spivey retorted, "You can only play for a hundred and this time you have to shoot for 210." (There are **only** 231 points on the table!)

Squirrel broke and put on another mind-boggling exhibition with a run of 20 balls. Squirrel ran all but one of the balls into his pocket to win again. Squirrel had made a monster one–pocket run of 41 balls under extraordinarily difficult conditions. It was a world-class performance in every regard.

Spivey paid up and said, "That's it for you, Squirrel. You're barred from the game."

Squirrel was the only player to beat Spivey's proposition until Harold Worst and Eddie Taylor came along.

Before long the ordinary professionals gave up on Spivey's challenge, so Brier offered an incentive. A One-Pocket run often depends on making one tough shot. If the player can pull off a near impossible bank or a razor thin table length cut with perfect position, there would be a very good chance of finishing the rack from there.

To even things up a bit Spivey allowed ordinary players to call upon any player they wanted to shoot ONE shot in each game.   A consensus chose Eddie Taylor for the tough banks and Harold Worst was the designated shooter for straight-in shots.

When either of these prodigious players was brought to the table and shown a near hopeless situation, they would solemnly nod and ask, "What do you want to shoot next?"

Then they proceeded to make a spine-tingling shot that no one else would dare try.

After losing a few sessions because of Worst and Taylor's interventions, Spivey barred them from substitute shooting.

Johnston City in the 1960s was a place of wonder and intrigue for pool players and spectators alike.

TICK TOCK

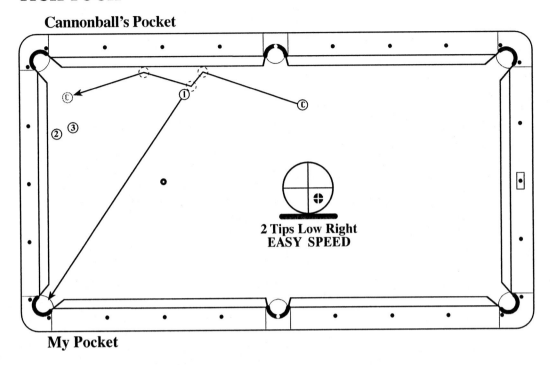

Cannonball's Pocket

**2 Tips Low Right
EASY SPEED**

My Pocket

Here's a shot I used to defeat the notorious "Cannonball Lefty" Chapman.

3 Cushion players call these "Tickies."

In situations where you can hide the Cue Ball behind a barricade like the 2-ball and 3–ball this is a strong Shot–Safety move. If the 1–ball drops, you are in the catbird seat ready to run the game out. If not, your opponent will have a problem to deal with.

Use **2 Tips of Low Right Draw** and **EASY SPEED**.

Cornbread Red and Me

The great, **Billy "Cornbread Red" Burge**, of Detroit, Michigan.

Cornbread Red liked to bet so high that it "put a tremble" in an opponent's stroke. Red was one of my heroes. Whenever I ran into him, I hung on to him the whole time. I was totally fascinated by him. I followed him everywhere but into the bathroom.

Red was another master at shooting off money balls. When confronted with the *big-cheese-money-ball*, Red would derisively snort, "Haw, haw," in his inimitable style, then he would increase his normally long back stroke about another foot, and *slip-stroke* the shot in, with dust flying out of the back of the pocket.

Red was unbeatable playing One-Pocket on a 5 x 10 snooker table. He was a great hustler, a great player, and a joy to watch — almost as funny as Minnesota Fats — a scandalous, shameless rogue, and I dearly miss him so.

VERNON ELLIOT'S INCREDIBLE CROSS CORNER BANK

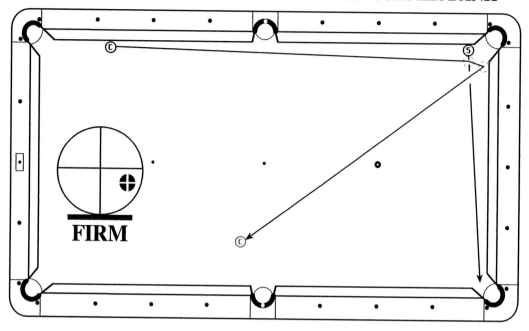

This amazing shot was made famous by **Vernon Elliot.**

Vernon only needed two tries to make this unbelievable bank shot and break all the smart guys in Johnston City in 1972.

Use extreme Right-English with a **FIRM** perfectly-timed, laser–accurate stroke.

VERNON ELLIOT'S MIND BUSTING CROSS SIDE

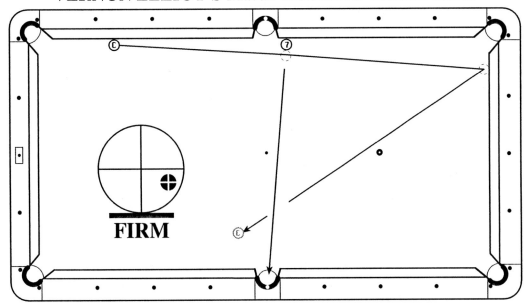

FIRM

Another psycho shot from Vernon Elliot.

This shot is even more difficult than the cross-corner because the Object Ball must be banked *backwards* to score. Nevertheless, Vernon made this brain-damaging cross–side shot within ten tries to rob unbelievers.

Extreme Right-English and a **FIRM** perfectly-timed, laser–accurate stroke is required.

3 Rails In Corner Off Spot

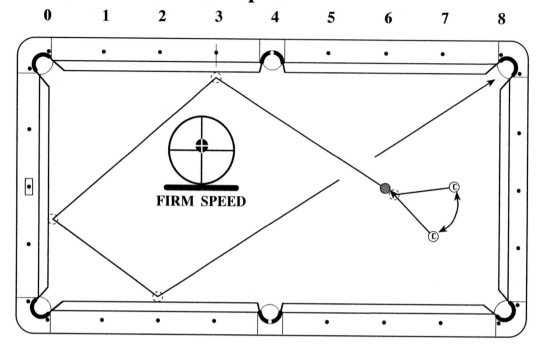

You can make a 3 cushion shot into the corner off the Foot Spot by hitting **OPPOSITE** Diamond 3.0 on the long rail using **FIRM SPEED**.

This bank works with **Cut, Passover** and **Straight On** shots.

FIVE RAIL ONE-POCKET SHOT

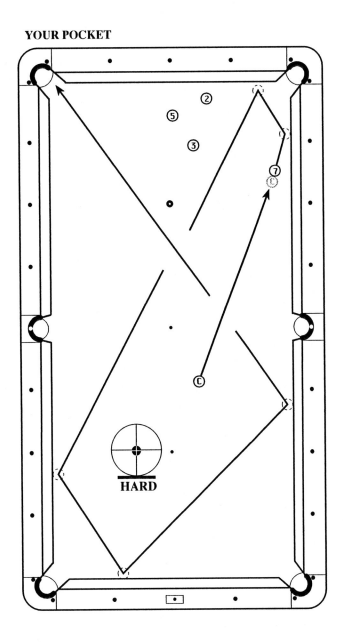

Bank the Object Ball five rails, **STOP** the Cue Ball and run the remaining balls.

Use Center Ball with a Hard Stroke.

Z–BANGERS

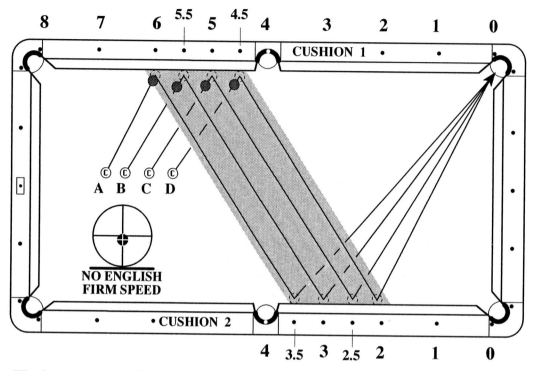

The key to making **Z–Bangers** is banking the Object Ball on the tracks shown here or **PARALLEL** to them.

It makes no difference whether the shot is a Natural Bank, a Cut Bank or a Passover Bank, any ball that can be played into the **GREY AREA** can be sent on a **Z–BANGER** path by banking the ball **PARALLEL** to these known shots instead of figuring a complicated formula.

OPTIMUM ANGLES

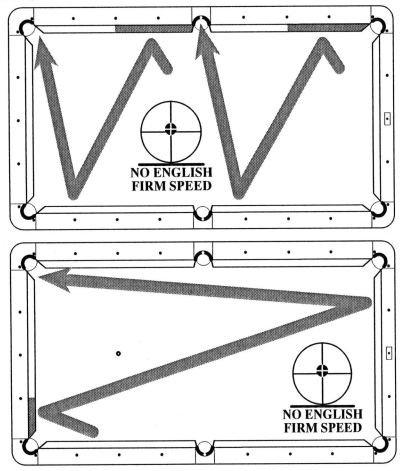

Natural Angle 2:1 banks can be successfully played two–rails using Firm Speed, No English at any point in the shaded areas. Just hit exactly on the Natural 2:1 Angle.

DOUBLE–KISS BANK

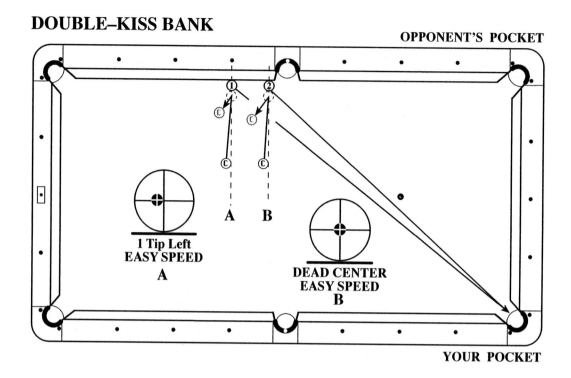

Both Object Balls are frozen to the cushion, but if these shots are hit slightly off–center or at a slight angle (as shown) you have a good chance of making the ball in your pocket or lagging it up near your pocket for a strategic move. The alignment for these shots should be about 1/2 Ball Space away from the direction of the bank.

RONNIE ALLEN KICK BANK

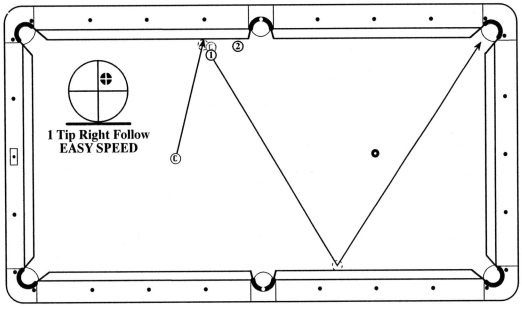

You didn't want to leave the mighty Ronnie Allen shots like this because most of the time he would kick–bank the 1–ball into his pocket, stop the Cue Ball for dead position on the 2-ball and run the game out.

If Allen happened to miss, his opponent faced a tough safety snookered behind the 2–ball.

BANKING WITH THE BEARD

EVADING A FOUL

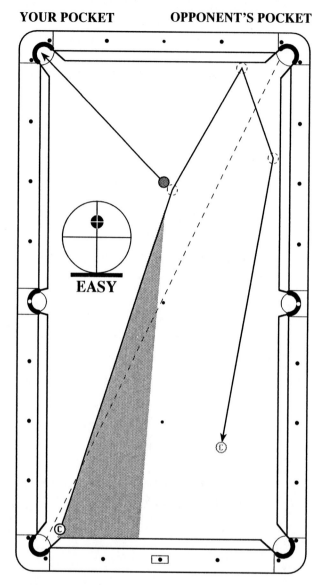

The Object Ball is on the Foot Spot.

You can confidently play this shot without a scratch as long as the Cue Ball is anywhere in the grey area.

Use Follow, No English, Easy Speed with a stop shot delivery (i.e. no follow-through).

AIR BRIDGE

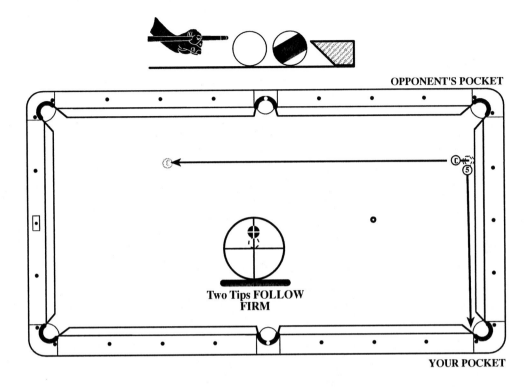

With the Cue Ball so close to the cushion there is a big risk of fouling on the rebound (i.e. double hit).

The secret is using a fist bridge with the bridge hand completely off the table the same as for a free-hand massé. The difference is that the cue is held level to the table rather than being perpendicular.

You must use follow so you can immediately raise the cue to avoid the Cue Ball coming back. Having the bridge hand off the table to begin with makes it possible to escape a foul.

JERSEY RED'S DOUBLE KISS

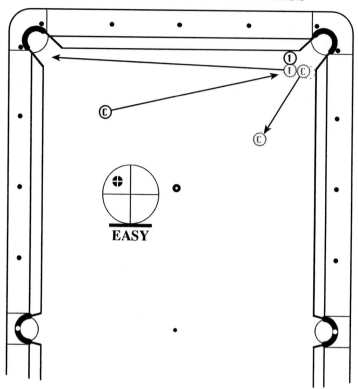

EASY

A One Pocket Solution

Jersey Red was even money to make this double kiss.

Use **Two Tips of High Left English** with a 1/4 ball hit on the right side of the Object Ball. Use **Soft Speed**.

The Cue Ball goes to the long rail and intercepts the rebounding Object Ball driving it into your corner pocket.

The Beard's Crunch Shot

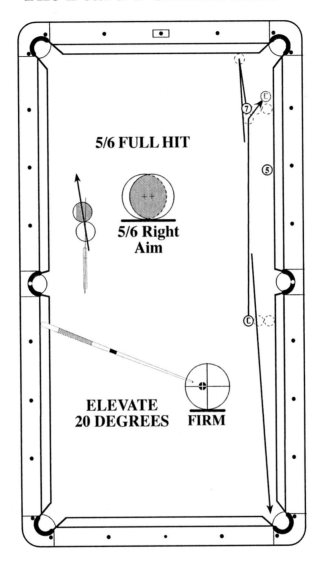

Use a **5/6 Full Hit**.

ELEVATE the cue about **20 degrees** and use **1 Tip Left-English.**

FIRM SPEED.

The Object Ball is cut slightly to the left, the english catches on the cushion and throws the Object Ball into the back pocket.

The Cue Ball ducks inside and sits on the rail for the out shot on the 5–ball.

CLIFF JOYNER'S CAROLINA EXPRESS

Here's a five star shot from **Cliff Joyner**. Cliff rarely missed one of these double-tough shots.

The shot begins with the Cue Ball and Object Ball one ball–space off the rail.

The difficulty lies in cutting the ball away from the cushion a bit to give the Cue Ball a carom angle to escape a kiss coming back and then overcoming the negative angle and **Collision–Induced–Throw**. Getting enough action on the Object Ball to send it back to the pocket is a challenge.

The gaff on this shot is to use **2-3 Tips Right-Hand English** on the equator of the Cue Ball with the **cue elevated 30 degrees**.

The Cue Ball leaves the table momentarily, eliminating friction from the cloth, so

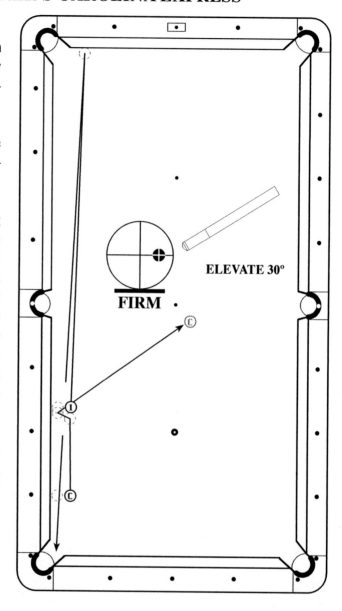

however much english you use is applied to the Object Ball. The slight bounce also helps the Cue Ball carom to the rail and out of the way of the 1-Ball coming back.

This bank belongs at the end of a Master Banker's Test. It is one of the most difficult banks even for top players.

COLE DICKSON'S HEARTBREAKER

Cole Dickson loved to shoot out of this One–Pocket trap using this trick bank.

Elevate the cue 30 degrees, hit below center with no english (you want the Cue Ball to leave the table slightly). By leaving the table, friction does not affect the Cue Ball and **Collision–Induced–Throw** kicks in on contact turning the Object Ball back to the pocket.

Use **Firm Speed**.

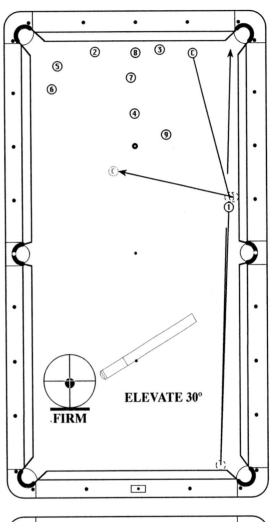

Everything is the same except the shot is on the short rail. You can pick up the Object Ball off the rail (but not if it is frozen to it) and bank it into the opposite pocket.

The trick is the same. Elevate and hit the Object Ball on the way down.

Use **Firm Speed**.

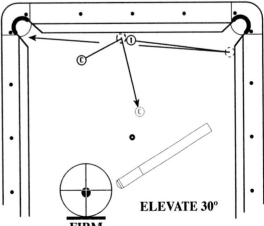

EDDIE TAYLOR'S KNOXVILLE SPECIAL

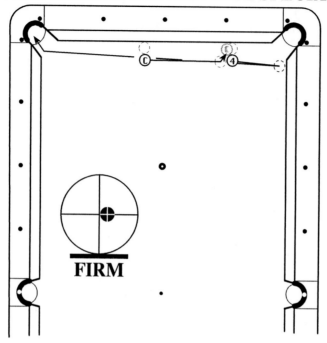

FIRM

Eddie Taylor didn't invent this shot, but he probably played it better than anybody.

Use **1 Tip Right-Hand English** with a level stroke. Firm Speed.

The Cue Ball ducks inside the Object Ball and lays against the rail while the Object Ball passes it going into the pocket.

Notice that the Cue Ball moves **Forward** about 1/2 Ball Space on successful attempts.

This is one of the most difficult banks, even for top players.

ANOTHER EDDIE TAYLOR MIND WRECKER

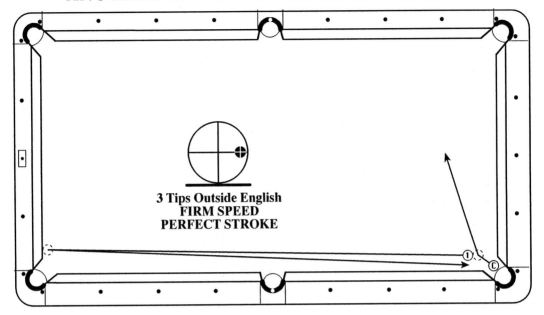

3 Tips Outside English
FIRM SPEED
PERFECT STROKE

Here's a great reply to a great safety.

Nicky Vachiano, from Philadephia, was a pretty good player and a very high roller.

Nicky once made a game with a top player where he could use the great Eddie Taylor to shoot all his bank shots.

This shot is much more difficult than it may appear because of the necessity of overcoming the **Collision–Induced–English** and **Throw** from this angle, so Nicky asked Taylor if the shot was possible.

Taylor responded, "Where do you want the Cue Ball?"

Use **3 Tips Outside English Firm Speed**.

This is an extremely difficult bank, even for the best bankers.

FROZEN OBJECT BALL

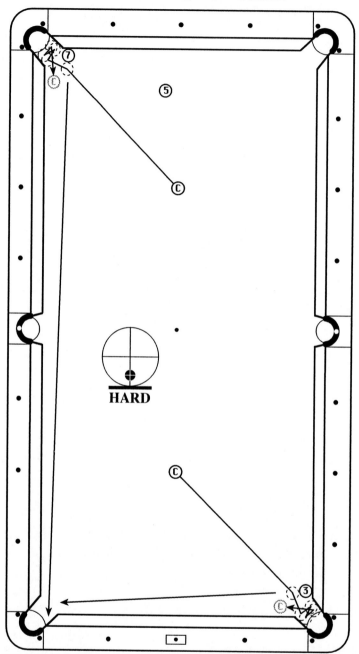

FROZEN OBJECT BALL

With the Object Ball frozen to the lip of the pocket, and the Cue Ball at a 45-degree angle, use **Hard Speed, Extreme Draw, No English** and a **1/4 Ball Hit**.

The Cue Ball rebounds several times inside the pocket to beat the kiss.

SMASHING AWAY A KISS

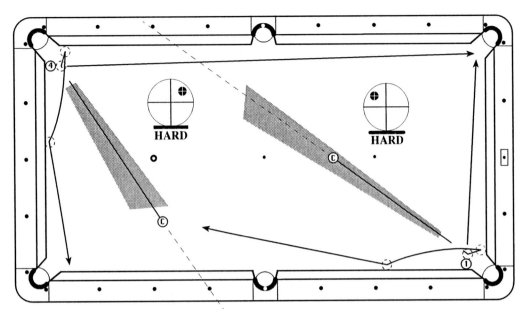

When this shot is lined up in the narrow range shown, you can bank the frozen ball cross corner without a kiss by using **Hard Speed** with **2 Tips of Outside Follow**.

The force of the shot sinks the Cue Ball into the cushion for an instant while the Object Ball escapes the kiss.

You should aim to hit the Object Ball *slightly* on the side toward the end rail as though you were banking the ball above the pocket. The angle of the shot applies enough **Collision–Induced–English** to turn the ball to the pocket.

A little experimentation will show you the proper angle for this shot. When the angle is right this is a fairly easy shot.

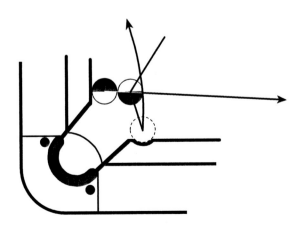

FORCE THRU OFF SPOT

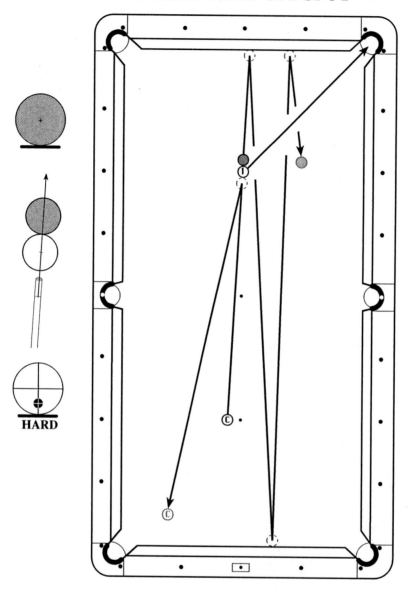

HARD

Place the Cue Ball slightly to the left of the Head Spot. Hit the Object Ball dead full in the face, using Extreme Draw with no english.

The 1–ball will drive through the second ball to score.

CROSS TABLE VERSION

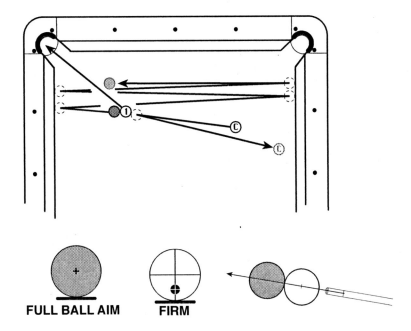

FULL BALL AIM **FIRM**

This often overlooked shot is basically the same as the more common force–thru off the spot on the preceding page.

Use Extreme Draw, Firm Stroke, No English.

1 RAIL ONE-POCKET SHOT–SAFETY

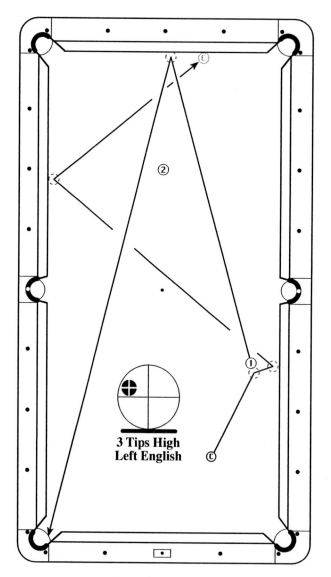

**3 Tips High
Left English**

Shoot with 3 Tips High Left-Hand English. **FIRM Speed**.

The Cue Ball travels 2 rails for a potential snooker behind the 2–ball and a tough leave on the end rail if the 1–ball fails to drop.

EXTREME 1 RAIL ONE-POCKET SHOT-SAFETY

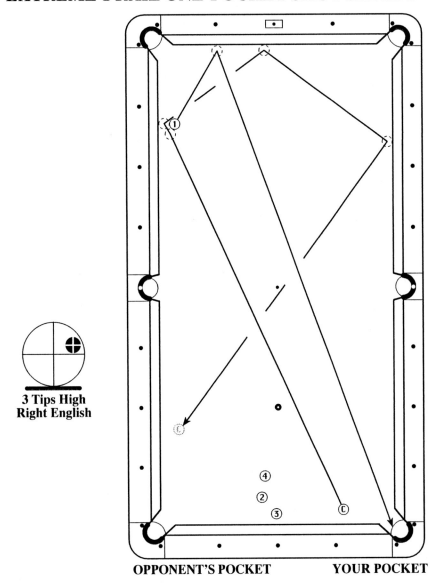

**3 Tips High
Right English**

OPPONENT'S POCKET   **YOUR POCKET**

Shoot with 3 Tips High Right-English. Paper thin hit, edge to edge aim.

The Cue Ball travels 3 rails for a Shot-Safety position where you can continue your run if the 1–ball scores while leaving the opposition a tough shot if you miss.

THE BEARD THROWS A CURVE

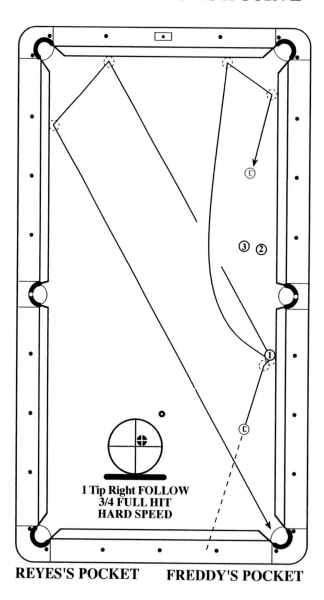

1 Tip Right FOLLOW
3/4 FULL HIT
HARD SPEED

REYES'S POCKET   **FREDDY'S POCKET**

Here's a nifty 3–Railer I used to run out a 1–pocket game against Efren Reyes.

Forced Follow action bends the Cue Ball path around the 2– and 3–balls for position to finish the game while sending the Object Ball 3 rails into my corner.

A fairly full hit is required to produce the overspin coming off the cushion to drive the Cue Ball around the 2– and 3–balls for a winning position.

A BUD HARRIS KICK SHOT

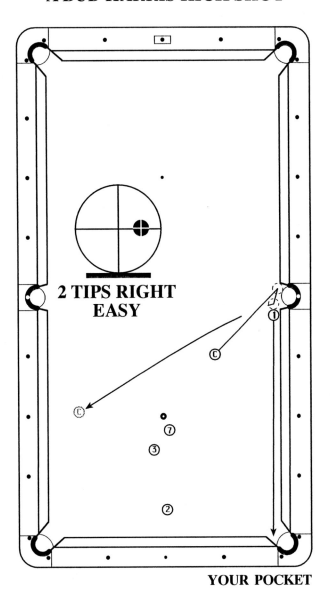

A lot of people play this shot nowadays, but when I learned it from Bud Harris no one knew it.

Hit the pocket facing with **2 Tips Right–English, Easy Speed**.

Practice and experimentation will show you how to play the shot.

2 RAIL FACING KICK SHOT

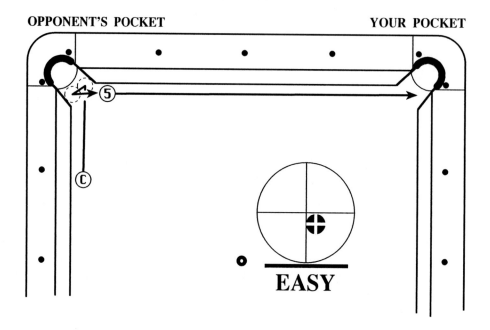

Here's a one-pocket kick that comes up from time to time.

Shoot directly into the pocket facing using 1 Tip Low Right-English with **Easy Speed**.

The Cue Ball rebounds off both pocket facings and kicks the Object Ball into the opposite pocket.

3 RAILS MY WAY

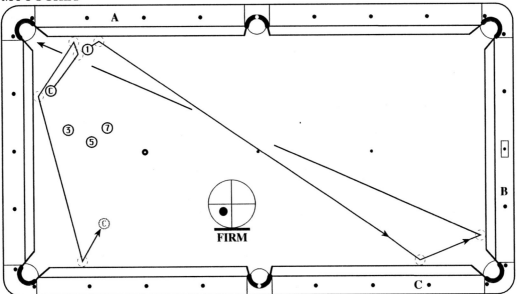

MY POCKET

OPPONENT'S POCKET

Most players try this 3 rail One–Pocket shot going to **Cushions A - B - C**. Here's my approach.

Going the wrong way — **A - C - B** — provides more latitude in speed for landing the Object Ball near your pocket.

Transferred English from the Cue Ball and *Acquired English* from contact with **Cushion A** deadens the Object Ball coming off **Cushions C** and **B** for a soft landing near my pocket if I miss.

Players unfamiliar with the wrong way bank think it is luck when you make the shot.

ONE-POCKET SITUATION

Opponent's Pocket

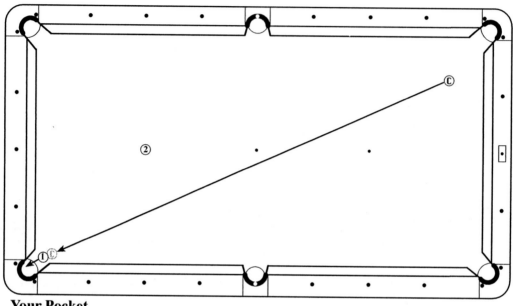

Your Pocket

You need two balls and the opposition needs one. Your opponent is shooting.

Shooting the ball on the Foot Spot would be a bad move, so your opponent makes your 1–ball and stops the Cue Ball leaving you hanging in the pocket.

Now you both need one ball to win.

What do you do from here?

ONE-POCKET SOLUTION

Opponent's Pocket

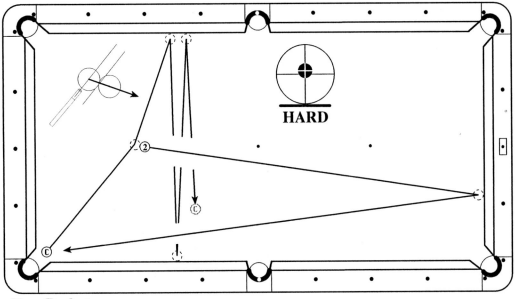

HARD

Your Pocket

You are buried in your pocket and you and your opponent each now need 1 ball to win.

With the last ball on the Foot Spot use an extreme edge to edge cut using **Hard Speed**.

A touch of high ball (1/2 Tip) helps eliminate the slide that would undercut the shot.

Do not use any side english. Using no side-spin allows you to beat the kiss when the Object Ball heads for the pocket.

3 Rails In Corner Adjustment

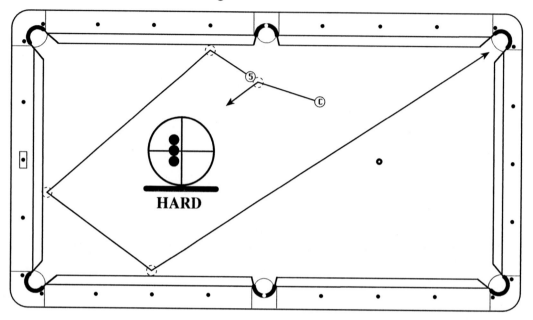

This shot has a propensity to come short into the long rail off the third rail.

SOLUTION:

Use **Reverse English** (Left-English this time) with a **HARD STROKE**.

Follow, Center and Draw work.

4 Rails In Corner Adjustment

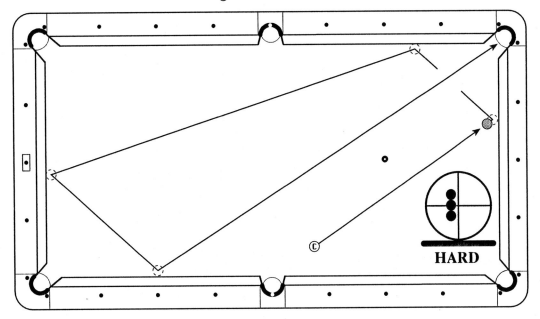

This shot also tends to run short off the fourth rail.

SOLUTION:

Use Reverse English (Left English in this case) with a **HARD STROKE**.

Follow, Center and Draw work.

MOST DANGEROUS BALL

In One-Pocket end game situations the most powerful ball for either player is a ball in front of the side pocket on his side. The reason being that this is the most difficult ball to move away.

It is a priority to move this ball away at the first opportunity

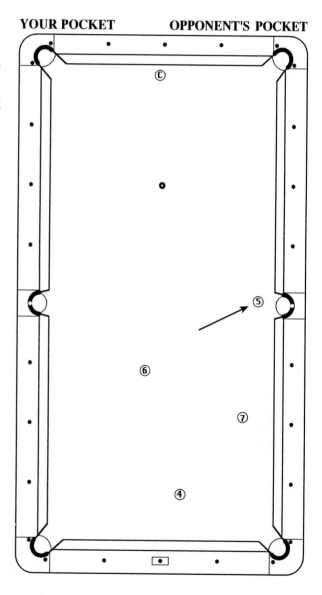

MOST DANGEROUS BALL

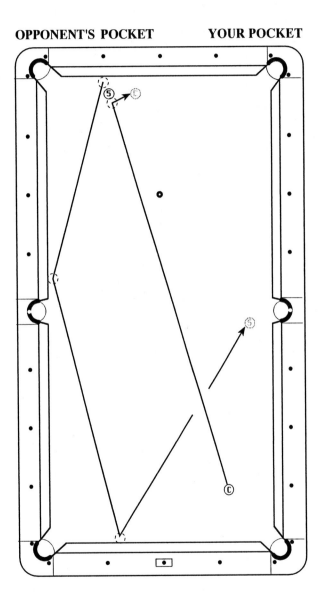

OPPONENT'S POCKET **YOUR POCKET**

Knowing this, it becomes imperative when driving a ball away from your opponent's pocket to try and place it in front of the side pocket on our side.

This is a very strong defending position because balls in front of side pockets present a multiple threat. First off there may be a scratch if the ball is played into the upper corner. If the ball is played in the side, it spots up and is difficult to play safe on.

TWICE CROSS-SIDE

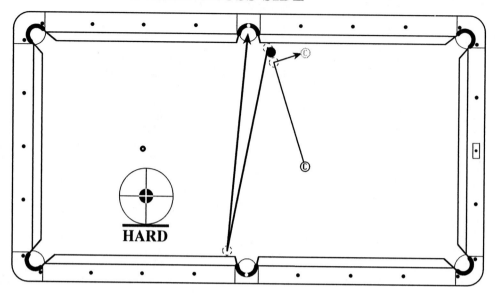

HARD

The difference between a 2–Rail and a 3–Rail shot is the **SPEED** you use.

To make this shot 2-Rails Cross–Side, cut the Object Ball slightly with no english and hit it **HARD**.

To make the shot 3–Rails Cross–Side, adjust the speed and hit the ball **FIRM**.

The shot below has always been one of my specialties. I was the first to shoot this bank consistently for the cash. Since then many good bankers have learned the shot, but I led the way.

THRICE CROSS-SIDE

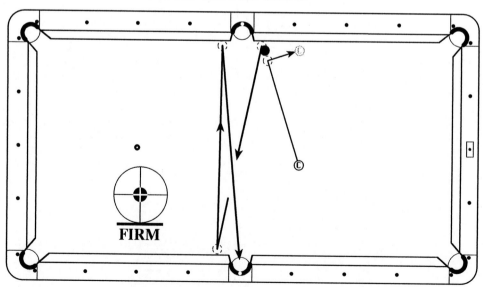

FIRM

FOUR RAILS CROSS SIDE

Use Center Ball, Hard Speed, 1/2 Full Hit. Level Stroke

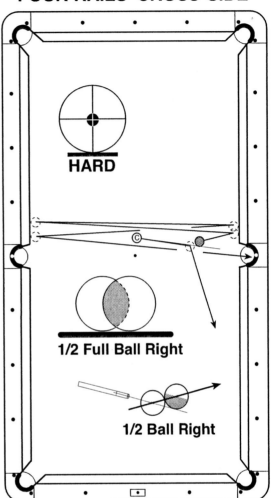

HARD

1/2 Full Ball Right

1/2 Ball Right

3 RAIL ONE-POCKET SHOT–SAFETY

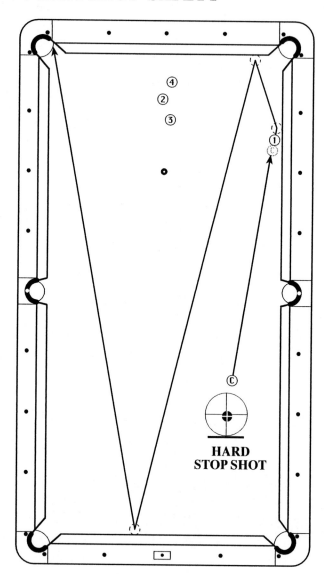

Shoot **HARD** and use **STOP SHOT** action. A small amount of draw is used to create the dead slide that stops the Cue Ball.

If you make the ball you run out.

If the 1–ball misses and lands near your pocket, it may block banks into your opponent's pocket.

Moreover, the 1-ball will be hidden behind the 2-3-4-ball barricade making a return safety more difficult.

**HARD
STOP SHOT**

CENTER BALL PINCH BANK

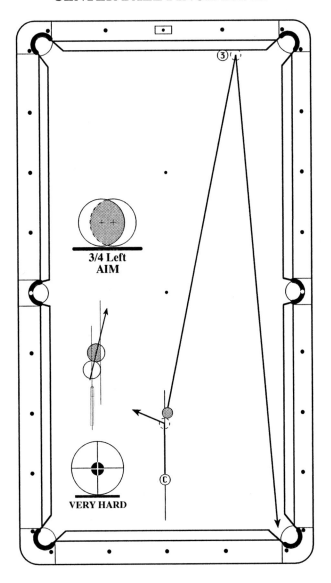

Use approximately a **3/4 Full Hit, Dead Center** — no left, no right and no top or bottom.   Use a perfectly level stroke for maximum slide.

Use a **Very Hard** delivery to carry the slide all the way to the cushion.

TWO or THREE CUSHION SHOT

BANK 1

The Cue Ball is slightly closer to the short rail than the Object Ball. The bank will not go **1-Rail**, but a **2-Rail** shot is a hanger.

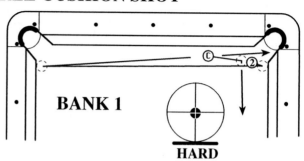

Cut the Object Ball enough to catch the long rail. Use a **Dead–Level Center Ball** stroke without english.

Shoot with **HARD** Speed.

To make the shot **3-Rails** use **Firm Speed**.

BANK 2

Identical except for the longer distance involved.

Cut the Object Ball just enough to catch the short rail and use a **Dead–Level Center Ball** stroke without english.

Shoot with **HARD** Speed.

To make the shot **3-Rails** use **Firm Speed**.

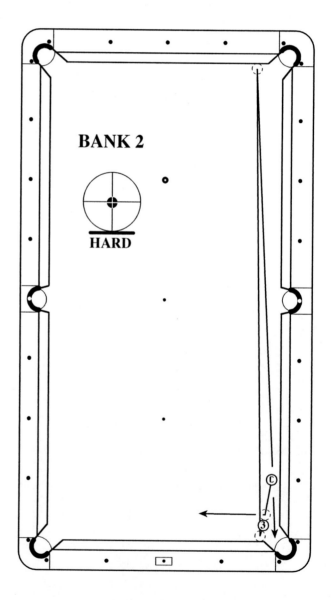

Rail First Cross–Corner

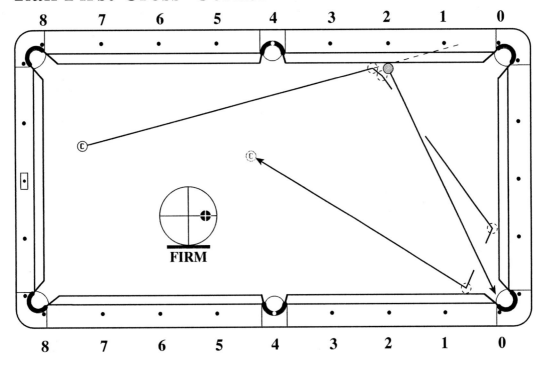

Here's an interesting way to beat a kiss.

Hitting cushion first with **2 Tips of Outside English** sends the Object Ball Cross–Corner and brings the Cue Ball back to the center of the table.

Freddy Bentivegna's DIAMOND PRO ACTION BANKS ™

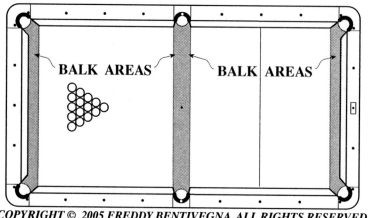

COPYRIGHT © 2005 FREDDY BENTIVEGNA ALL RIGHTS RESERVED

SPEEDO BANK RULES

1. Fifteen balls are racked and must be broken wide open like nine ball. Safe breaks are not allowed. If a ball is made on the break without a scratch, the ball(s) is spotted and the shooter continues.

2. Draw lines between the points of the two side pockets. Then draw lines between the outer points of the corners on each short rail. These are the 3 balk areas.

3. After the break, balk area spot up rules go into effect, as follows:

    a.   Spot all balls that lie inside the 3 balk areas.

    b.   Any ball touching a balk line is considered in balk.

    c.   Balls made on the break are spotted immediately. All other balls are spotted after each shooter's inning.

    d.   After the breaker's inning, continue to spot up balls that lie in the balk areas, all balls pocketed illegally and any balls that jumped the table.

    e.   These rules remain in effect as long as there are 8 or more balls on the table.

    f.   When there are 7 balls or less in play, the game reverts to standard **BANK POOL** rules, where balls are spotted normally and the balk rules are discontinued.

4. **Nine Ball Banks**: All the above rules apply except that the balls required to nullify the balk area spot up rules is reduced to 5 instead of 8.

Freddy Bentivegna's DIAMOND PRO ACTION ONE POCKET ™

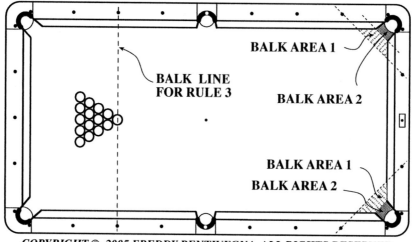

BALK AREA 1

BALK LINE
FOR RULE 3

BALK AREA 2

BALK AREA 1

BALK AREA 2

COPYRIGHT © 2005 FREDDY BENTIVEGNA ALL RIGHTS RESERVED

SPEEDO One–pocket RULES

1. Draw a balk line from diamond one on long rail to diamond one on short rail on both sides of the table. This will be designated *Balk Area 1*.

    a. Spot up the balls that land in that space as long as you have 8 or more balls on the table.

    b. A ball *touching* a balk line is *in* balk.

2. Draw another set of diagonal balk lines between the points of the back corner pockets. This will be designated *Balk Area 2*.

    a. When there are *less* than 8 balls on the table the balk area recedes to the smaller space between the points of the corner pockets, designated *Balk Area 2*, and we now spot only the balls that lie in that smaller space.

3. When there are 8 balls or more on the table and they have all traveled past the second diamond at the foot of the table, the 3 balls closest to the head rail are to be spotted up except in cases where balls are in balk. Balls in balk will always have precedence in the spotting order.

    a. If a ball is pocketed in a non–scoring pocket by the outgoing player, it is placed on the foot spot and that in itself constitutes a ball outside the balk area and no other balls need to be spotted.

b. If more than 3 balls qualify to be spotted up, the order of preference is:

(1.) Any ball pocketed in a neutral pocket

(2.) All balls within *Balk Area 2*

(3.) All balls within *Balk Area 1*.

(4.) Balls closest to the back rail.

(5.) If balls are equally located the low numbered ball is spotted.

c. No more than 3 balls can be spotted altogether.

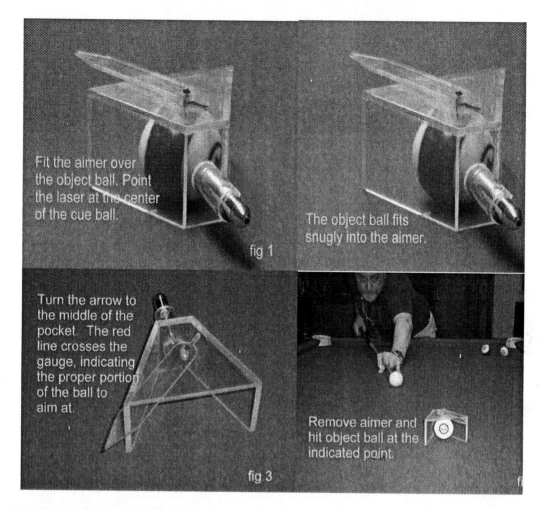

Fit the aimer over the object ball. Point the laser at the center of the cue ball.

fig 1

The object ball fits snugly into the aimer.

Turn the arrow to the middle of the pocket. The red line crosses the gauge, indicating the proper portion of the ball to aim at.

fig 3

Remove aimer and hit object ball at the indicated point.

The Beard's DEAD–EYE AIMER
Trademark reg# 09621
9 January 2004

The operation of this unit is simple. Place the unit over the Object Ball. It is built to fit perfectly. Turn on the laser and point it to the center of the Cue Ball. Next, turn the swing arm on top of the unit so as to be pointing to the center of the designated pocket. Note the calculation that the line on the arm crosses over. That will be your aiming point on the Object Ball. (i.e., 1/4 ball full, 1/2 ball full, 3/4 ball full, etc.) The aiming point is an exact calculation as opposed to other aiming systems that employ erroneous "imaginary Cue Balls" as the basis for their system. My system is the only one that allows for "**Collision-Induced-Throw**" on the Object Ball.

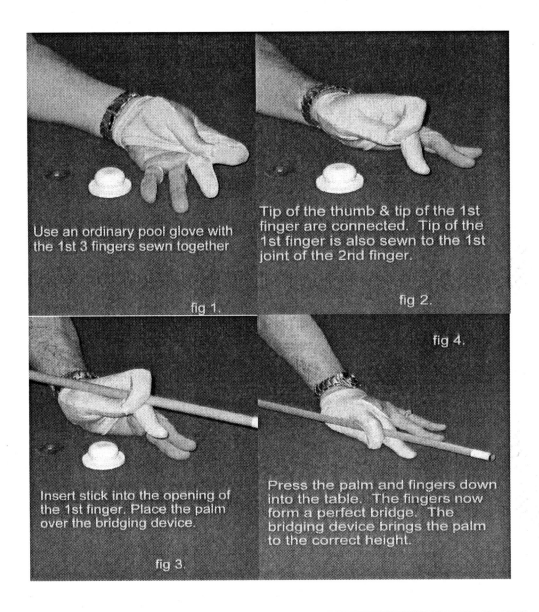

Use an ordinary pool glove with the 1st 3 fingers sewn together

fig 1.

Tip of the thumb & tip of the 1st finger are connected. Tip of the 1st finger is also sewn to the 1st joint of the 2nd finger.

fig 2.

fig 4.

Insert stick into the opening of the 1st finger. Place the palm over the bridging device.

fig 3.

Press the palm and fingers down into the table. The fingers now form a perfect bridge. The bridging device brings the palm to the correct height.

The Beards PRO BRIDGE MAKER
TRADEMARK REG # 091198
1 August 2003

NEW ORDERS
BANKING WITH THE BEARD
$29.95 + $4.00 S & H

PHONE　　—　　1—312—225—5514

ONLINE — www.BANKINGWITHTHEBEARD.COM

MAIL　CHECK OR MONEY ORDER　TO　BANKING WITH THE BEARD
445 West 27th Street
Chicago, IL 60616

Printed in the United States
35397LVS00004B/70

9 780976 622819